T0294913

Banking the Unbanked

CalAccount Market Study and Feasibility Assessment

Jonathan W. Welburn | Robert Bozick |
Maya Buenaventura | David Metz |
Vegard Nygaard | Patricia K. Tong |
Kelsey O'Hollaren | Jessie Coe | Jessie Wang |
Lane F. Burgette | Katherine Burnham |
Jim Mignano | Shannon Prier | Natalie Cox |
Chandra Garber | Anujin Nergui |
Kami Ehrich | Elizabeth Marsolais |
Samuel Absher | George Zuo |
Rakesh Pandey | Lily Hoak |
Nicolas M. Robles |
James Syme |

Sponsored by the
California State Treasurer's Office

RAND

For more information on this publication, visit **www.rand.org/t/RRA3117-1**.

This report was updated in August 2024 to reflect changes based on public comments, as described in Annex III, Appendix J.

About RAND

RAND is a research organization that develops solutions to public policy challenges to help make communities throughout the world safer and more secure, healthier and more prosperous. RAND is nonprofit, nonpartisan, and committed to the public interest. To learn more about RAND, visit www.rand.org.

Research Integrity

Our mission to help improve policy and decisionmaking through research and analysis is enabled through our core values of quality and objectivity and our unwavering commitment to the highest level of integrity and ethical behavior. To help ensure our research and analysis are rigorous, objective, and nonpartisan, we subject our research publications to a robust and exacting quality-assurance process; avoid both the appearance and reality of financial and other conflicts of interest through staff training, project screening, and a policy of mandatory disclosure; and pursue transparency in our research engagements through our commitment to the open publication of our research findings and recommendations, disclosure of the source of funding of published research, and policies to ensure intellectual independence. For more information, visit www.rand.org/about/research-integrity.

RAND's publications do not necessarily reflect the opinions of its research clients and sponsors.

Cover image: Front: Adobe Stock/peterschreiber.media (bank card), Adobe Stock/Onchira (motion blur peeps); Back: Adobe Stock/ Travellaggio (trees)

Image credits: page IV: Adobe Stock/VK Studio; page VI: Adobe Stock/suzyanne16; page IX: Adobe Stock/ Zamrznuti tonovi; page X: Alamy Stock/Rodolfo Arpia; page XII: Alamy Stock/Paul Briden; page 2: Alamy Stock/Jeffrey Isaac; page 4: Alamy Stock/ZUMA Press Inc; page 7: Adobe Stock/Kim Britten; page 12: Adobe Stock/Hugh O'Neil; page 14: Adobe Stock/Rafael Ramirez; p. 21- Adobe Stock/ Thares2020; page 24: Adobe Stock/amnaj: page 26: Adobe Stock/jetcityimage; page 27: Adobe Stock/Pefkos; page 28: Adobe Stock/ master1305; page 29: Adobe Stock/Olga; page 35: Adobe Stock/Savannah1969; page 37: ronstik; page 40: Adobe Stock/Юля Бурмистрова; page 42: Adobe Stock/muji; page 47: Adobe Stock/Syda Productions; page 52: Adobe Stock/Zamrznuti tonovi; page 56: Alamy Stock/DPD ImageStock; page 60: Adobe Stock/rocketclips; page 62: Adobe Stock/Brastock Images

ABOUT THIS REPORT

The California Public Banking Option Act, enacted in October 2021, established the CalAccount Blue Ribbon Commission (the Commission) and required the Commission to deliver a market analysis to determine whether it is feasible to implement a "CalAccount Program." The California State Treasurer's Office selected RAND to carry out the feasibility study by

- conducting a survey of Californians who may be unbanked or underbanked
- documenting fees charged by banks, credit unions, and alternative financial service providers (e.g., check cashing)
- market analysis of the landscape of banking options available to Californians
- analyzing current and potential bank branch locations in relation to population demographics
- analyzing the quantitative and qualitative costs and benefits of the CalAccount Program
- analyzing the potential impacts of the CalAccount Program on historical disparities
- assessing the feasibility of the CalAccount Program and requirements for its operations.

This report documents our research, methods, and findings.

This work was sponsored by the California State Treasurer's Office. The study team was led by principal investigator Jonathan Welburn and project director Robert Bozick; task leads Maya Buenaventura, David Metz, Vegard M. Nygaard, Patricia K. Tong, and Jessie Wang; and project manager Elizabeth Marsolais. For all inquiries, email CalAccountProject@rand.org.

RAND Social and Economic Well-Being

RAND Social and Economic Well-Being is a division of RAND that seeks to actively improve the health and social and economic well-being of populations and communities throughout the world. This research was conducted in the Social and Behavioral Policy Program within RAND Social and Economic Well-Being. The program focuses on such topics as risk factors and prevention programs, social safety net programs and other social supports, poverty, aging, disability, child and youth health and well-being, and quality of life, as well as other policy concerns that are influenced by social and behavioral actions and systems that affect well-being. For more information, email sbp@rand.org.

Acknowledgments

This report is a product of tremendous insights from numerous individuals that extend beyond the project team. We are thankful to the four peer reviewers—Philip Armour, Katie Fitzpatrick, Angela Hung, and Aaron Strong—for their thorough reviews, considered feedback, and thoughtful suggestions throughout this project. We are grateful to our RAND colleagues, including Beverly Weidmer and the RAND Survey Research Group for their expertise and hard work in fielding the RAND California Survey of Household Finance, and Julia Rollison, RAND Social and Behavioral Policy Program Director, and Anita Chandra, RAND Vice President for Social and Economic Well-Being, for their leadership and advice. We are grateful to the numerous individuals beyond RAND who have provided key inputs to our study. We are thankful to survey participants and to subject-matter experts whose insight shaped our findings and to the members of the CalAccount Blue Ribbon Commission and the CalAccount Advisory Council for their feedback and advice throughout this project. We are thankful to Marco Lizarraga and Dora Angulo from La Cooperativa Campesina de California, who helped connect us with migrant farmworkers to include in our survey. Finally, we are thankful to the California State Treasurer's Office, which sponsored this work; to Mariah Ramos for her administrative support; and to our project officer, Cassandra DiBenedetto, who provided consistent support and feedback.

Summary

The California Public Banking Option Act, enacted in October 2021, established the CalAccount Blue Ribbon Commission ("the Commission") and required the Commission to deliver a market analysis to determine whether it is feasible to implement a "CalAccount Program," which the state would establish to provide Californians access to a voluntary, zero-fee, zero-penalty, federally insured transaction account and related payment services at no cost to accountholders. The program would also need to include mechanisms for accessing account funds and account management tools that automate basic financial transactions designed to serve the needs of individuals with low or fluctuating income.

In April 2023, the Commission asked RAND to conduct the legally required feasibility study. To respond to the legislative language, we undertook a study organized into several tasks:

1. understanding the financial services landscape in California—including both banking and alternative financial services—with respect to geographic location and fees

2. understanding who are the unbanked and underbanked in California and what is their access to and use of banking and alternative financial services

3. examining the feasibility of key CalAccount requirements and related obstacles

4. conducting a benefit-cost analysis (BCA) framed around three potential options for CalAccount.

CALIFORNIA'S LANDSCAPE FOR BANKING AND BANKING ALTERNATIVES

To conceptualize California's banking landscape and landscape for banking alternatives, we collected data from 418 banking institutions, of which 153 are commercial banks (5,629 branches) and 265 are credit unions (1,567 branches). Within this sample, we see a strong correlation between population count and branch density, with commercial banks and credit unions (collectively referred to as *traditional banks*) mostly located in and around major cities. We found that most Californians who live in cities have good access to branch offices with only small difference among racial and ethnic groups in cities. In less densely populated areas of the state, particularly for rural Native Americans, we found that access to branch locations is more challenging. For fees charged by banks and alternative financial service providers, we found the following:

- Most credit unions and commercial banks require minimum deposits to open an account.

- Monthly service fees are common, costing about $8 on average at commercial banks

- Overdraft fees are common, with over 95 percent of banks charging a minimum of $15.

- Check-cashing fees vary with the check amount.

- Money order fees range from $0.60 to $4.00, with limits between $500 and $1,000.

- Prepaid cards often incur multiple fees, including monthly, transaction, automatic teller machine (ATM) withdrawal, and reloading fees.

v

UNBANKED AND UNDERBANKED CALIFORNIANS

To understand the financial management practices of unbanked and underbanked Californians, with the goal of assessing their receptivity toward a potential CalAccount program, we analyzed data from two sources: the *2021 FDIC National Survey of Unbanked and Underbanked Households* ("the FDIC survey") and the RAND California Survey of Household Finance ("the RAND survey"), which was administered between January and April of 2024 and developed so that the results can be generalized to the populations of unbanked and underbanked California households.

RAND Survey Responses

Responses to the RAND survey suggest that the CalAccount Program may address some concerns of unbanked households, such as minimum balance requirements. However, other leading reasons for not having a bank account, such as not needing one because of low funds or preferring cash transactions, would not be addressed by the program. The survey results also indicate that levels of trust in government and financial institutions are higher among the underbanked than among the unbanked. Importantly, the RAND survey indicates that overall interest in opening a bank account is relatively low among the unbanked, with less than half expressing interest. Key features that could attract the unbanked and underbanked to open accounts include no minimum balance requirements and having physical bank locations. Yet even with these features, a majority of the unbanked appear hesitant to open an account.

Definitions of *Unbanked* and *Underbanked*

We define unbanked households and underbanked households in alignment with the parameters used by the FDIC in its biennial surveys on banking administered by the U.S. Census Bureau.

Unbanked households are those in which none of the members has a checking or savings account at a bank or credit union.

Underbanked households are those in which one of the members has a checking or a savings account at a bank or credit union, but a member of the household also used an alternative financial service in the past 12 months. These alternative financial services include money orders, check-cashing services at places other than a bank, money transfer services, payday loans, pawn shops, tax-refund anticipation loans, and automobile title loans.

Disparities

Data from the 2021 FDIC survey show that while the overall unbanked rate in California was 5.1 percent in 2021 and the underbanked rate was 13.9 percent, disparities existed in unbanked and underbanked rates by race and ethnicity. For example, the unbanked and underbanked rates of non-White households were more than double rates of White households, as were the rates of Hispanic households compared with White non-Hispanic households.

Other disparities we noted included that married households had lower unbanked and underbanked rates than unmarried households and that underbanked rates for households in metropolitan statistical areas (MSAs) were lower than the rates of households not in MSAs. In contrast, unbanked rates for households in MSAs are higher than households not in MSAs.

The disparities in unbanked and underbanked rates are greatest between low-income households (those with less than $30,000 in annual household income) and non-low-income households. The unbanked rate for low-income households was six times the rate of non-low-income households, and the underbanked rate for low-income households was almost twice that for non-low-income households.

FEASIBILITY OF KEY CALACCOUNT FEATURES

Using an approach that combined a document review and stakeholder interviews, we examined the feasibility of the key components of CalAccount described in the California Public Banking Option Act, including the proposed nine-member CalAccount board, required account features, and enrollment of individuals who lack a federal or state government-issued photo ID and individuals without permanent housing. We also considered feasibility challenges not directly related to these key components and provided recommendations for overcoming feasibility challenges. Table S.1 summarizes our findings on the feasibility of CalAccount features.

In considering feasibility, we note that all the primary CalAccount features (with the exception of requiring registered payees to limit late fees) are similar or identical to transaction account features already being offered through alternatives accounts similar to CalAccount, such as Bank On-certified banks and MoCaFi/Sunrise Banks, N.A.

CalAccount will be feasible only if at least one FDIC-insured bank is willing to participate in the program. However, offering no-fee accounts, at scale, may not be profitable (or even cover the basic costs of account maintenance) and may not, on its own, provide ample incentive to banks to participate in CalAccount. Additionally, perceived legal liability risks may be a further barrier to bank participation. Finally, enrollment may be one of the largest challenges for CalAccount feasibility, as both lack of interest in having a bank account and lack of trust in banks and government among California's unbanked underbanked populations are meaningful barriers.

Table S.1 | Account Features and Feasibility Concerns

Feature	Feasibility Concerns
Individuals who lack state or federal picture ID, are unhoused, ages 14–18 can enroll	No major feasibility concerns.
Zero-fee, zero-penalty	Offering low- and no-fee accounts at scale may not be profitable from a bank's perspective, so banks may have little incentive to promote these accounts.
Federally insured	No major feasibility concerns.
Connectivity with other state and local government programs	No major feasibility concerns, but fraud issues in other government programs highlight the importance of investment in fraud prevention technologies and processes.
Payroll direct deposit	No major feasibility concerns
Registered payees	From a practical standpoint, utility companies and other entities may choose not to register as payees because of the late-fee limitation.
Electronic funds transfer for deposits and rent	No major feasibility concerns.
Nine-member board	No major feasibility concerns.

EXPLORING POLICY OPTIONS: COSTS, BENEFITS, AND TRANSFERS

We modeled policy options for CalAccount to evaluate the relative cost-effectiveness of potential structures the program might take. These options are presented as hypothetical scenarios intended to reflect the scope and magnitude of potential social and economic impacts of CalAccount under different sets of assumptions regarding the general structure of the program (see Table S.2). For each option, we conducted a BCA as a useful framework to evaluate and compare investments or policy decisions.

Benefit-Cost Analysis Findings

Our findings suggest that the success of CalAccount hinges most on enrollment. If CalAccount does not reach a sufficient level of uptake, costs are likely to outweigh benefits. If it does, benefits are likely to outweigh costs, including meaningful savings for customers and significant reductions in unbanked disparities.

We estimate that the societal benefits from CalAccount could outweigh its costs over a decade if enrollment is adequate. The program mainly benefits unbanked and underbanked households in California through savings from avoided fees. However, nonmonetary might include improvements in

Table S.2 | Potential Costs, Benefits, and Transfers Associated with Policy Options for CalAccount

	Option 1: Mobile Banking	Option 2: Mobile Banking + Existing Brick-and-Mortar Financial Network	Option 3: Mobile Banking + Expanded Brick-and-Mortar Financial Network
Expected enrollments	Low	High	Highest
Size of financial network	Access to a robust and geographically expansive ATM network, with limited or no access to in-person banking	Access to a robust and geographically expansive ATM network, including bank or credit union branches	Access to a robust and geographically expansive ATM network, including bank or credit union branches plus additional state-designated locations
Potential costs	• Outreach • Enrollment • Account maintenance • Issuing debit cards • Customer service • Direct deposit service	Option 1 costs *plus* • ATM hardware and software • Interface with state systems	Option 2 costs *plus* • Identifying and assessing new markets/customer segments • Monitoring and evaluating impact • Lease/construction • Office equipment/furniture • Staffing and training to support expanded financial network
Potential benefits	• Increased access to financial services • Safety of account holders • Accrued savings • Entrepreneurship • Building financial history • Potential revenue to banks through return-on-deposits and interchange fees	Option 1 benefits *plus* • Access to in-person banking options	Option 2 benefits *plus* • Access to enrollment options or other program support in certain state/local government buildings (or other locations)
Potential transfers	• Other fees (e.g., overdraft, check-cashing, payday loans) • Monetary transfers to CalAccounts		

financial inclusion, literacy, stability, and innovation. While participating banks and the state could also benefit from new deposits and revenue-sharing, the program's operational costs might be too high to incentivize bank participation without subsidy.

Furthermore, our BCA shows that a network of physical bank branches offers the greatest net societal benefits, whereas a mobile-only banking option is limited by potential access issues. An expanded network, including nontraditional locations, offers the highest benefits but the smallest net benefit because of staffing costs. Using distributional weights to focus on social well-being changes the analysis, showing positive net benefits across all policy options and ranking the expanded network highest, suggesting a focus on increasing enrollment and access over cost-effectiveness to maximize societal benefits.

RECOMMENDATIONS

Based on our findings, we offer policymakers the following four recommendations to support a sustainable CalAccount Program.

- **Implement CalAccount with instant payments.** Mandating faster payments, which would provide account holders faster access to their funds, may reduce reliance on check-cashing services.[1]

- **Leverage low-cost options for in-person services including enrollment.** Although access through ATM networks and existing branches may suffice for some unbanked and underbanked households, where new locations are needed, particularly in rural areas, using existing government facilities (such as post offices and municipal buildings) and mobile bank branches may extend access in a manner that increases uptake while managing potential costs.

- **Maximize awareness using community partners.** Such partnerships may be crucial to reaching the level of enrollment that would allow CalAccount to succeed.

- **Consider an implementation study.** Our study points to several key areas in need of additional analysis, including developing a better understanding of trust concerns, considering how best to integrate community partners, and refining potential options for CalAccount's structure. An implementation study could be conducted before or during program implementation.

IX

NOTE

[1]   Ryan C. McDevitt and Aaron Sojourner, "The Need for Speed: Demand, Regulation, and Welfare on the Margin of Alternative Financial Services," *Review of Economics and Statistics*, January 2023.

Contents

Summary..v

Introduction...1

Banking and the Unbanked and Underbanked in California....................5

Feasibility Review of Key CalAccount Components.............................25

Options for CalAccount 41

Discussion and Conclusion 57

Available at www.rand.org/t/RRA3117-1

Annex I: The State of Banking in California

- Appendix A: Analyzing the California Banking Landscape
- Appendix B: CalAccount Legal Issues

Annex II: Potential Benefits, Costs, and Impacts of the CalAccount Program

- Appendix C: Benefit-Cost Analysis
- Appendix D: Modeling CalAccount Take-Up
- Appendix E: Impact of CalAccount on Disparities and Savings
- Appendix F: The Potential Impacts of CalAccount on Longer-Run Benefits, Public Safety, and Banks

Annex III—RAND California Survey of Household Finance Methodology

- Appendix G: Survey Description
- Appendix H: Survey Instrument
- Appendix I: Crosswalk Between Report Contents and Contract Requirements
- Appendix J: Public Comment

chapter
1

Introduction

The California Public Banking Option Act, enacted in October 2021, established the CalAccount Blue Ribbon Commission (the Commission) and required the Commission to deliver a market analysis to determine whether it is feasible to implement a "CalAccount Program."[1] CalAccount would be established by the state to offer Californians access to a voluntary, zero-fee, zero-penalty, federally insured transaction account and related payment services at no cost to account holders. The California Public Banking Option Act stipulates that the program would also need to include robust and geographically diverse mechanisms for accessing account funds and account management tools that facilitate the automation of basic financial transactions designed to serve the needs of individuals with low or fluctuating incomes.

In April 2023, the Commission asked RAND to conduct a feasibility study that would do the following:

- determine whether it is feasible to implement a CalAccount Program with all the characteristics mentioned in the legislation

- indicate whether there are modifications to the CalAccount Program that can ease the implementation burdens

- determine whether CalAccount Program revenue, largely drawn from debit card interchange fees and fractional reserve lending, is more likely than not to be sufficient to pay for CalAccount Program costs within six years of the CalAccount Program's implementation

- determine the population of California residents who are unbanked and the reasons they are unbanked

- determine the low-cost or no-cost options of federally insured transaction accounts that are available or marketed to unbanked California residents

- evaluate CalAccount Program alternatives

- recommend how the state can maximize the number of unbanked California residents who become banked at the lowest cost and risk to the state

- analyze the relative advantages and disadvantages, compared with private-sector alternatives, that the

1

Definitions of *Unbanked* and *Underbanked*

We define unbanked households and underbanked households in alignment with the parameters used by the Federal Deposit Insurance Corporation (FDIC) in its biennial surveys on banking administered by the U.S. Census Bureau.

Unbanked households are those in which none of the members has a checking or savings account at a bank or credit union.

Underbanked households are those in which one of the members has a checking or a savings account at a bank or credit union, but a member of the household also used an alternative financial service in the past 12 months. These alternative financial services include money orders, check-cashing services at places other than a bank, money transfer services, payday loans, pawn shops, tax-refund anticipation loans, and automobile title loans.

state may have in identifying, reaching, or persuading unbanked California residents to enroll in a state-administered banking program

- interview relevant subject-matter experts (SMEs) from the banking industry, legal and regulatory communities, organizations reflecting customer needs, and the academic and research communities that study banking and financial inclusion

- recommend an appropriate governance structure for a public-private partnership such as the CalAccount Program

- analyze costs, benefits, and impacts on all affected parties, including, but not limited to, landlords, employers, state government, low-wage workers, and consumers

- evaluate other "important considerations."

2

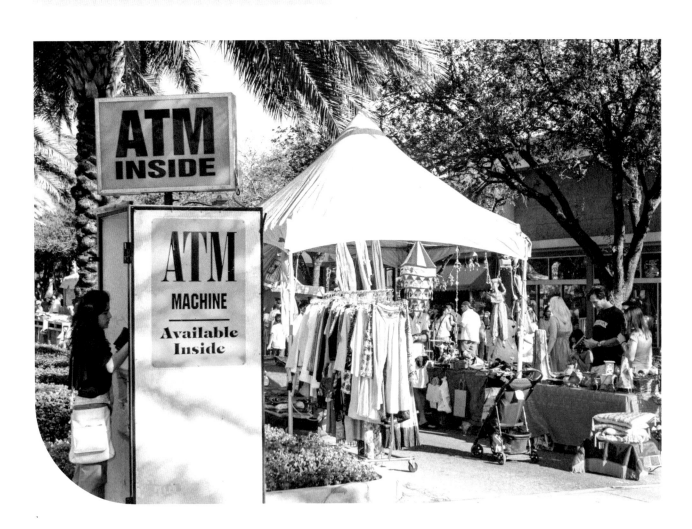

To respond to the legislative language, we undertook a study that we organized into the following tasks:[2]

1. understanding the financial services landscape in California—including both banking and alternative financial services—with respect to geographic location and fees

2. understanding who are the unbanked and underbanked in California and what is their access to and use of banking and alternative financial services.

3. examining the feasibility of key CalAccount requirements and several related obstacles

4. conducting a benefit-cost analysis (BCA) framed around three potential options for CalAccount.

ORGANIZATION OF THIS REPORT

In Chapter 2, we provide overviews of the landscape for banking and banking alternatives and of the unbanked and underbanked population in California. In Chapter 3, we describe our analysis of the feasibility of the key components of CalAccount. In Chapter 4, we discuss broadly the expected benefits and costs of CalAccount, noting that some impacts associated with the public good can be hard to measure, and then we apply those considerations to three options for implementing the program. We conclude in Chapter 5 with a discussion of the comparative advantages and disadvantages of each policy option, and we highlight additional feasibility issues, lay out study limitations, and offer recommendations for California policymakers.

We provide more-detailed discussions of our analyses, including respective methodologies, in the appendixes to this report, which are available at www.rand.org/t/RRA3117-1:

Annex I: The State of Banking in California

- Appendix A: Analyzing the California Banking Landscape
- Appendix B: CalAccount Legal Issues

Annex II: Potential Benefits, Costs, and Impacts of the CalAccount Program

- Appendix C: Benefit-Cost Analysis
- Appendix D: Modeling CalAccount Take-Up
- Appendix E: Impact of CalAccount on Disparities and Savings
- Appendix F: The Potential Impacts of CalAccount on Longer-Run Benefits, Public Safety, and Banks

Annex III: RAND California Survey of Household Finance Methodology

- Appendix G: Survey Description
- Appendix H: Survey Instrument
- Appendix I: Crosswalk Between Report Contents and Contract Requirements
- Appendix J: Public Comment.

Abbreviations

AB	Assembly Bill
ATM	automated teller machine
BCA	benefit-cost analysis
BSA	Bank Secrecy Act
CBO	community-based organization
CIP	customer identification program
DFPI	California Department of Financial Protection and Innovation
FDIC	Federal Deposit Insurance Corporation
FFIEC	Federal Financial Institutions Examination Council
FinTech	financial technology
ID	identification
KYC	Know Your Customer
MSA	metropolitan statistical area
NCUA	National Credit Union Administration
NPV	net present value
NSF	nonsufficient funds
OMB	U.S. Office of Management and Budget
PV	present value
SME	subject-matter expert

NOTES

[1] California State Legislature, California Public Banking Option Act, AB 1177, October 4, 2021. The law amended Title 21.1 of the Government Code, commencing with Section 100100, to establish the Commission.

[2] Our study was originally composed of five tasks: a survey, an analysis of the banking landscape in California, a benefit-cost analysis, an impact analysis, and assessment of CalAccount operations.

chapter
2

Banking and the Unbanked and Underbanked in California

The state of banking in California is the product of the market for banking services and demand for those services. In this chapter, we analyze that market, including fees associated with banking institutions and alternative financial service providers before discussing RAND survey findings on demand for banking services.

THE BANKING AND FINANCIAL SERVICES LANDSCAPE IN CALIFORNIA

Commercial Banks and Credit Unions

One of the main goals of CalAccount is to offer fee-free checking accounts. To better understand the implications of such a program, we start by examining how checking account fees vary across the banks and credit unions that currently offer this service in California.

Our analysis looked at all active commercial banks insured by the Federal Deposit Insurance Corporation (FDIC) and all active credit unions insured by the National Credit Union Administration (NCUA) that have a physical branch in California and offer personal checking accounts (also referred to as *share draft accounts* by credit unions). Our final sample includes 418 institutions, of which 153 were commercial banks (5,629 branches) and 265 were credit unions (1,567 branches). Below, we summarize our findings on the landscape of banking in California; we provide extensive details in Appendix A.

Figure 2.1, which provides a map of the branch locations in California and the total population for each zip code in the state, shows the strong correlation between population count and branch density, with commercial banks and credit unions (collectively referred to as *traditional banks*) mostly located in and around major cities, such as Los Angeles, San Diego, San Francisco, and Sacramento. Most Californians who live in cities have good access to branch offices as measured in terms of physical proximity. About one-quarter of the population that lives in cities reside more than 1 mile from a branch office, and only 4 percent reside more than 2 miles from the nearest branch.

A comparison across demographic groups shows small differences in banking access for certain minorities living in cities, with 29.3–31.7 percent of the Black, Hispanic, and Native American population residing more than a mile from the nearest branch, compared with 25.7–26.8 percent for

5

Figure 2.1 | Bank and Credit Union Branch Locations and Population Size, by Zip Code

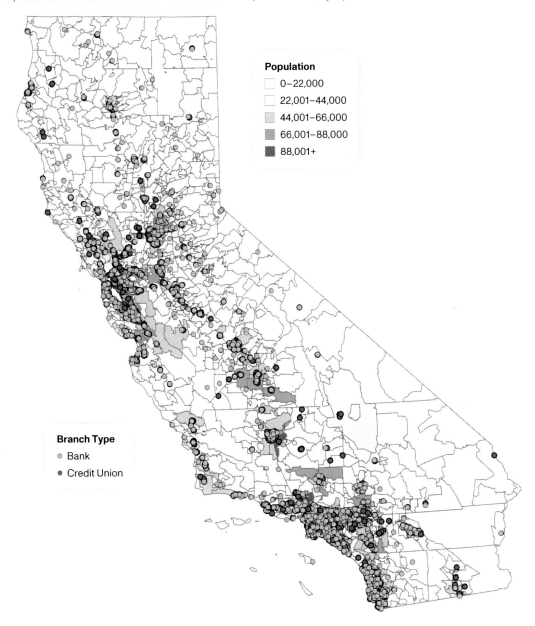

SOURCE: Commercial bank branch locations are from FFIEC, undated-c (data accessed on January 29, 2024). Credit union branch locations are from the NCUA, 2024b (using data from September 2023).

NOTE: Only institutions that have at least one physical branch in the state and that offer personal checking accounts are included. *Population* refers to total population in the zip code.

Asian American and White Californians. Banking access is more challenging in less densely populated areas of the state, particularly for Native Americans who reside rurally, with nearly one-third of this demographic group residing more than 10 miles from the nearest branch office and about 10 percent residing more than 20 miles away.[1]

While our analysis of banking access is based on physical proximity to branch locations, we do not intend to draw false equivalence in location and access to all banking services. In some cases, we note that mobile banking access is strengthened by other government-sponsored efforts, such as the Broadband Equity Access and Deployment (BEAD) Program. However, even with equal access to branch locations, further disparities can exist. Notably, a 2022 study from the Roosevelt Institute sent canvassers to 106 bank branches across California to analyze whether low-cost banking options were made available to prospective customers.[2] The study found that that a majority of canvassers were not told of low-cost banking options when they were available and that significantly higher rates of minority canvassers were turned away from banks (30 percent for those of color and 40 percent for those who were Spanish speaking) in comparison with White canvassers (4 percent). While our analysis sought to construct a comprehensive dataset of banking fees rather than observe disparities in access, our experience suggests that finding the lowest-cost account offered by a bank would be a challenge for regular customers, with some banks promoting only their higher-cost accounts. Moreover, we found that several institutions report their fees on various disclosure forms that are likely not understandable to all customers and that can be difficult, and sometimes impossible, to locate on an institution's website, thereby making it harder for Californians to compare checking accounts across commercial banks and credit unions. Additionally, while disparities in access to credit may exist, we did not assess credit and lending access, because those services will not be offered by CalAccount.

Monthly Service Charges, Overdraft Fees, and Minimum Deposit Requirements

We collected data on fees and minimum balance requirements for the basic checking account offered by each institution. (These data were obtained directly from the website of each commercial bank and credit union. Missing data were obtained through phone calls with customer representatives. Some credit unions were unwilling to disclose any information until they had verified that the prospective customer was eligible to join the credit union. Similarly, some banks were unwilling to disclose any information on the phone and required that prospective customers visit them at a branch location to obtain information about their services. Note that the fees that traditional banks charge can differ from the fees that we report because institutions sometimes update their fees. We collected the traditional banking fee data during fall 2023 and spring 2024.)

By *basic checking account*, we specifically mean a non-interest-bearing account that allows the customer to make purchases both in-store and online using a debit card linked to the account, pay bills, deposit and withdraw cash at automated teller machines (ATMs), and receive online direct deposits (e.g., to receive paychecks). This is generally the lowest-cost account offered by traditional banks.

Our data collection revealed that such accounts are rare in California. Among the 418 traditional banks we examined, only two offer checking accounts with no minimum opening deposit requirement, no monthly service charge, and no overdraft fee. (However, other fees that we did not collect data on, and that would not be charged by the proposed CalAccount Program, might still apply to their accounts.)

As shown in Figure 2.2, about one-fifth of commercial banks that operate in California provide checking accounts with no monthly service charge. Most, however, charge such fees, with a median fee of $7.88 and a minimum fee of $12 per month for the banks in the top 10 percent of this fee distribution.[3] Conversely, most credit unions do not charge monthly service fees for their basic checking accounts. Although about one-third of the credit unions charge such fees, the fee is generally lower than for commercial banks and is less than $10 for nearly all credit unions in our sample.

Traditional banks often offer ways to waive the monthly maintenance fee, hence, the *de facto* service charge difference between banks and credit unions (assuming the customer qualifies for the waiver) is lower than what is reported in Figure 2.2. Among the sample of traditional banks that charge a monthly maintenance fee, more than

Figure 2.2 | Unweighted Sample Distributions of Monthly Service Charges, Overdraft Fees, and Minimum Deposit Requirements

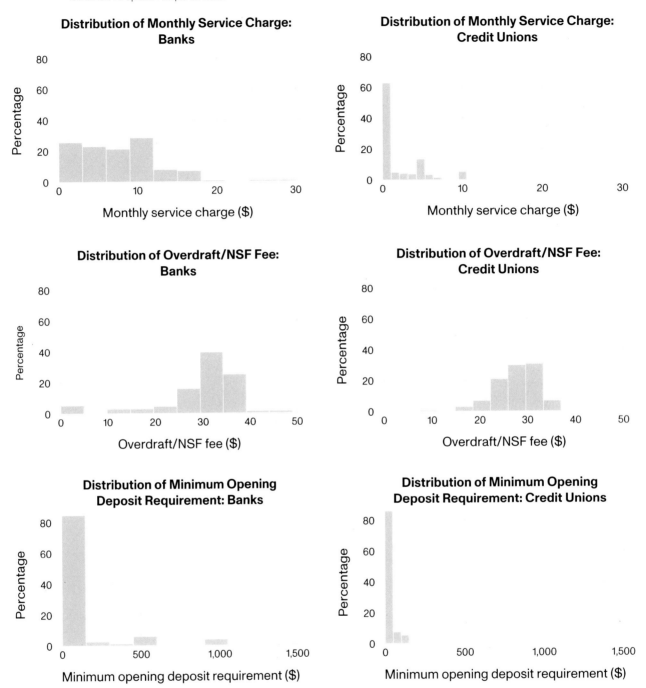

SOURCE: Primary data collection from the institution's website or from phone call with customer representative.

NOTE: All institutions are equally weighted to illustrate how the fees vary across the banks and credit unions that offer personal checking accounts in California.

90 percent allow for ways to waive the fee, the most common option of which is to maintain a sufficiently high account balance. For credit unions that provide this option, the monthly minimum balance requirement ranges from $50 to $2,500. The corresponding balance requirement for commercial banks that offer this option ranges from $100 to $10,000. A large share of institutions also waive this fee, either partially or in full, if the customer opts to receive their monthly statements electronically or by having monthly direct deposits that exceed a certain threshold.

Most traditional banks charge overdraft or nonsufficient funds (NSF) fees for transactions that exceed a customer's account balance. Overdraft fees are levied when traditional banks cover the transaction, thereby leading to a negative account balance,[4] whereas an NSF fee is levied when a check is returned or a payment cannot be made because of insufficient funds. Most institutions charge an overdraft or NSF fee of $25–$35 per transaction ($0–$49 for commercial banks and $10–$37 for credit unions).[5] Following an overdraft, customers might also be charged exorbitant interest penalties that sometimes compound daily until they restore their account to a positive balance.

Note that some institutions limit the number of overdraft fees that customers can be charged daily, and some also provide a grace period to bring an account back to a positive balance before levying an overdraft fee. Several institutions allow customers to pay for an *overdraft protection* plan that enables funds from another linked account, such as a savings account, to be automatically transferred to cover transactions that exceed the customer's checking account balance. Although a few institutions do not charge overdraft fees, customers are still liable for potential interest penalties that accrue as long as the account balance remains negative. Repeat overdrafts may also result in involuntary account closures. Such involuntary account closures have long been common in the United States, with 6.4 million accounts involuntarily closed in 2005, nearly all of which were due to repeated overdrafts and NSF activities.[6]

Minimum deposit requirements, which apply only at the time the customer opens the account, are different from the minimum balance that several institutions require to waive a monthly service charge. The minimum opening deposit for the commercial banks in our sample ranges from $0 to $1,500, with a median of $100. In contrast, nearly half the credit unions in our sample do not require minimum

opening deposits for their basic checking account; however, prospective customers at credit unions cannot open a checking account until they have opened a savings account with the same institution. While the minimum deposit requirement for savings accounts varies across credit unions, it mostly ranges from $5 to $25. Additionally, we note that these savings accounts can also come with monthly service charges. While most of them do not, a subset of credit unions charge about $5 per month for their savings accounts. Unlike for banks, prospective customers at credit unions must also pay a nonrefundable membership fee, most commonly at a cost of $5, before they can open any account with the institution.

Nontraditional Banking and Payment Services

As noted in Chapter 1, the FDIC classifies a household as underbanked if it has a checking and/or savings account yet still uses alternative financial services regularly used by the unbanked population. To better understand the cost to Californians of using alternative banking and payment services, we collected data from nonbank vendors on fees for the following financial services: check cashing, money orders, money transfers, and prepaid debit cards.

Fees for check-cashing services generally scale with the value of the check. Because a large share of unbanked and underbanked households in the United States tend to be lower income, we focused on the costs of cashing a $100 check and a $500 check. As shown in Figure 2.3, the fee to cash a $100 check ranges from $1 to $10 in our sample, with a median fee of $2.25. The corresponding fee to cash a $500 check ranges from $1 to $50, with a median of $6.75 and a fee of at least $12.50 among the top 10 percent of the sample.

Money orders are routinely used by unbanked and under-banked households because they are a secure way to send money. They can result in large cumulative expenses. Among the sampled vendors, money order fees range from $0.60 to $4.00 per order, with a maximum amount of $500–$1,000 per order.[7]

General-purpose prepaid debit cards function like conventional debit cards and can be used to make online and in-store purchases and to pay bills. They can be reloaded with additional funds, albeit potentially at a cost to the consumer. Nearly all prepaid cards also come with additional fees, the most common of which are illustrated in Figure 2.4.

9

For example, although the majority of prepaid cards do not have monthly fees, those that do come at a high cost, with fees of $5 per month for the top 10 percent of the sample. Furthermore, while most prepaid cards do not charge per-transaction fees, 25 percent of them charge at least $0.50 per transaction. Similar to conventional debit cards, consumers can withdraw funds from their prepaid cards at ATMs. Doing so at out-of-network ATMs, however, generally incurs fees. Compared with traditional banks, which generally do not charge to deposit funds in a checking account, reloading prepaid cards usually has associated costs, with a median fee of $4.95. Most prepaid cards also charge balance inquiry and inactivity fees.

Among the prepaid cards in our sample, the median has seven fees in addition to those listed in Figure 2.4. Hence, although prepaid cards might provide a substitute for some of the services that banked consumers can access, these fees show that they generally come at a considerably higher cost to users.

Finally, we collected data on the cost of nonbank money transfer services. Both banked and unbanked households sometimes use these services to make international money transfers, for example, for remittances. Given the demographics in California, we collected data on the cost of a $1,000 money transfer to Tijuana, Mexico, and found there is almost no variation in this fee in our sample, with nearly all vendors charging $10 for this service.

Figure 2.3 | Sample Distribution of Check Cashing and Money Order Fees

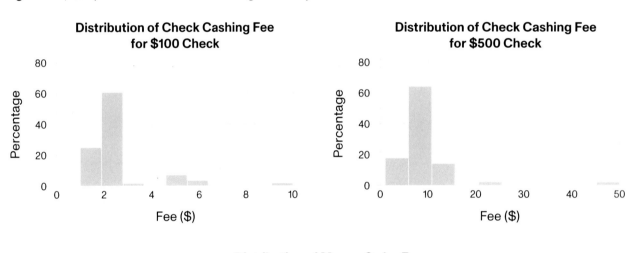

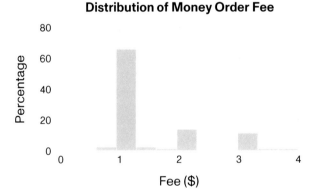

Figure 2.4 | Sample Distribution of Prepaid Card Fees

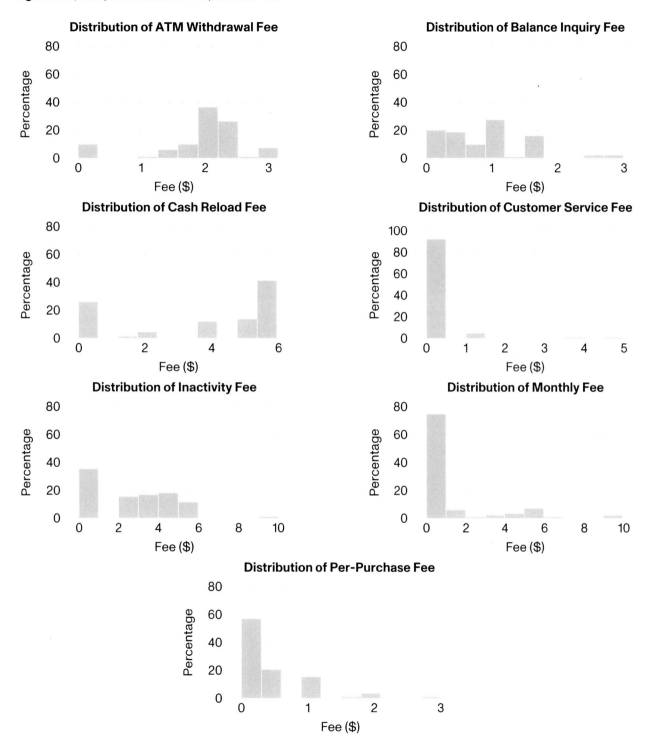

UNBANKED AND UNDERBANKED CALIFORNIANS

Key Demographic Details

To understand the financial management practices of unbanked and underbanked Californians, with the goal of assessing their receptivity toward a potential state-run CalAccount program, we analyzed data from two sources: the 2021 *FDIC National Survey of Unbanked and Underbanked Households* (i.e., "the FDIC survey") and the 2023 RAND California Survey of Household Finance (i.e., "the RAND survey"), which was administered between January and April of 2024 and developed so that the results can generalize to the populations of unbanked and underbanked California state residents.[8]

The FDIC survey is a biennial supplement to the U.S. Census Bureau's Current Population Survey. This survey is based on a nationally representative sample of households in the United States and includes a series of questions aimed directly at those who are unbanked or underbanked. In contrast to the FDIC, the RAND survey includes only residents in California who are unbanked or underbanked. (More details on our survey methodology are available in Appendix G.)

Throughout this report, we present findings from both the FDIC survey and the RAND survey. However, in cases where both surveys ask the same or similar questions, we prioritize the RAND survey because it is more recent, it includes modified question wording and response options specifically tailored to the aims of this feasibility study, and it has

more precision owing to a larger sample size of California's unbanked and underbanked residents. Additionally, the FDIC survey is an address-based survey, and consequently under-samples those living in accessory dwelling units, temporary group quarters, and recreational vehicles/trailer parks. As a consequence, the FDIC disproportionately omits migrant workers—a target population for the CalAccount Program. To overcome this limitation of the FDIC survey, the RAND survey includes a subsample of migrant farmworkers to augment its address-based sample.

Table 2.1. shows the demographic composition of both the FDIC and RAND surveys.[9] We break out the RAND sample by banked status, but we show the full sample for the FDIC survey because of its smaller sample size. Both surveys are household-based, meaning that they sample households and invite one household member to report on behalf of the rest of the members. The demographic characteristics in Table 2.1 are those of the sample respondent. In the following sections, we present key findings from this survey, including reasons cited by the unbanked for not having a traditional bank account, the types of financial transactions being made by the unbanked and underbanked and the various mobile and web-based services they use, and the likelihood of unbanked and underbanked individuals opening different types of accounts and their level of trust in institutions and financial services. In the figures that follow, we indicate in the source notes whether the analyses reflect household-level estimates or sample member-level estimates.

Disparities in Banking Among Californians

Data from the FDIC survey show that while the overall unbanked rate in California in 2021 was 5.1 percent and the underbanked rate was 13.9 percent, there are disparities in these rates by race and ethnicity and other demographic characteristics, as shown in Table 2.2. The percentages of non-White households that are unbanked or underbanked are more than double those of White households, and the percentages of Hispanic households that are unbanked or underbanked are more than double those of White non-Hispanic households.

Disparities also exist by household structure and residence in a metropolitan statistical area (MSA). Unbanked and underbanked rates are lower for married households than for unmarried households. Unmarried female households and unmarried male households have similar underbanked rates,

Table 2.1 | Key Demographic Characteristics of FDIC Survey and RAND Survey Sample Households (unweighted)

Characteristic	FDIC Survey California Subsample — Total Unbanked and Underbanked	RAND California Survey of Household Finance		
		Total Unbanked and Underbanked	Unbanked	Underbanked
Sex				
Female	48.7%	53.3%	52.6%	53.6%
Male	51.3%	41.6%	41.7%	41.6%
Prefer not to say	NA	5.1%	5.8%	4.8%
Race/Ethnicity				
Hispanic	46.0%	57.8%	52.9%	60.4%
White	25.3%	13.4%	9.5%	15.5%
Black	11.5%	12.6%	20.1%	8.7%
Asian	16.3%	2.9%	1.2%	3.8%
Other	0.9%	13.3%	16.4%	11.6%
Age (mean)	49.9	46.0	46.5	45.8
Nativity				
Native-born	51.1%	35.2%	28.9%	38.3%
Foreign-born	48.9%	59.6%	65.0%	56.9%
Prefer not to say	NA	5.2%	6.1%	4.8%
Educational attainment				
12th grade or less	23.1%	26.6%	36.5%	21.6%
High school graduate	31.7%	33.6%	35.1%	32.9%
Some college	21.4%	22.8%	19.7%	24.4%
Bachelor's degree	23.8%	8.5%	2.6%	11.6%
Employment status				
Employed	55.5%	49.3%	35.5%	56.3%
Unemployed	5.5%	10.0%	13.7%	8.2%
Not in the labor market	39.0%	40.7%	50.8%	35.5%
Sample				
Address-based sample	100.0%	92.5%	93.4%	92.1%
Migrant farmworker sample	0.0%	7.5%	6.6%	7.9%
N	454	1,034	348	686

SOURCE: Authors' tabulations using data from the FDIC and RAND surveys.

Characteristic	Unbanked Households		Underbanked Households	
	Number	Percentage	Number	Percentage
Race				
White households	449,276	6.9%	199,393	3.1%
Non-White households	1,575,267	19.5%	536,179	6.6%
Ethnicity				
Hispanic households	1,033,152	22.7%	348,622	7.7%
Non-Hispanic households	991,391	9.9%	386,949	3.9%
Household structure				
Married households	899,818	13.4%	247,896	3.7%
Unmarried male households	493,922	14.1%	242,648	6.9%
Unmarried female households	622,333	14.4%	238,769	5.5%
MSA status				
Households in MSAs	1,944,907	13.9%	712,410	5.1%
Households not in MSAs	79,636	14.9%	23,161	4.3%
Household Income				
Low-income households	634,926	21.8%	439,081	15.0%
Non-low-income households	1,389,617	11.9%	296,491	2.5%
Total			2,024,543	13.9%

SOURCE: Authors' tabulations using data from the FDIC and RAND surveys.

NOTE: Tabulations are weighted by household weights. Low-income are households with less than $30,000 in annual household income, and non-low-income households are those with incomes above $30,000. The table excludes migrant households.

but unmarried female households have lower unbanked rates than unmarried male households. Underbanked rates are lower for households in MSAs than for households not in an MSA. In contrast, unbanked rates in MSAs are higher than for households not in MSAs.

Disparities in unbanked and underbanked rates are greatest between low-income and non-low-income households, where *low-income household* is defined as a household with less than $30,000 in annual income. The unbanked rate for low-income households is 15.0 percent, which is six times the rate of households that are not low-income. The underbanked rate for low-income households is 21.8 percent, which is just under double the underbanked rate for households with annual income above $30,000.

Reasons for Not Having a Traditional Bank Account

Figure 2.5 illustrates the wide variety of reasons that unbanked households in the RAND survey cited for not having a bank account. Two of the three reasons given by a majority of unbanked households cannot be directly addressed by the CalAccount Program: not having enough money to need a bank account and preferring to handle transactions with cash. The third reason cited by a majority of unbanked households—which could be solved by CalAccount—was not having enough money for a minimum balance.

Figure 2.5 | Reasons Reported by the Unbanked for Not Having a Commercial Bank or Credit Union Account

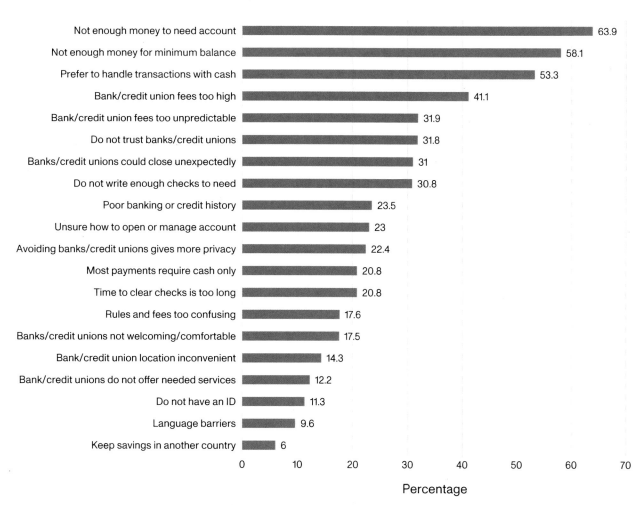

SOURCE: RAND California Survey of Household Finance (*n* = 343 unbanked sample members).

Financial Transaction Methods of the Underbanked and Unbanked

Figure 2.6 shows the preferred payment instruments for paying bills by banked status among households in the RAND survey sample. Among the underbanked, the most popular method was to use a check or debit card linked to a bank account. By definition, no unbanked household indicated this as their preferred method of payment. Conversely, the unbanked were nearly five times more likely than the underbanked to prefer cash payments, money orders, or cashier's checks to pay their bills. Furthermore, the unbanked were nearly 20 times more likely than their underbanked counterparts to indicate the use of "other" methods to pay their bills.

Underbanked and unbanked households also differed in their preferred methods for receiving funds from their work, retirement, and government funds, as shown in Figure 2.7. Strikingly, unbanked households were nearly 20 times more likely to prefer payment by cash, roughly seven times more likely to prefer payment by prepaid debit card, and almost twice as likely to prefer paper check payments relative to underbanked households. In contrast, just over two-thirds of underbanked households preferred payments be routed directly to their bank account.

Intrafamily transfers, such as remittances, are important financial transactions for Californians.[10] As shown in Figure 2.8, among unbanked households in the RAND survey, just under half preferred completing these transfers using cash. The most preferred method among the underbanked for intrafamily transfers were online or via mobile payment apps.

As with many other activities, there were large differences between the unbanked and the underbanked when it comes to their preferred payment instrument for making purchases (see Figure 2.9). Cash was the most popular method for making purchases among unbanked households, at roughly 47 percent, while the analogous figure for underbanked households was 12.2 percent. The second most preferred method for purchases among the unbanked was "other." Underbanked households, however, said that they most commonly purchase goods and services with check or debit cards connected to a personal bank account.

Figure 2.6 | Method Most Often Used to Pay Monthly Bills, by Banked Status

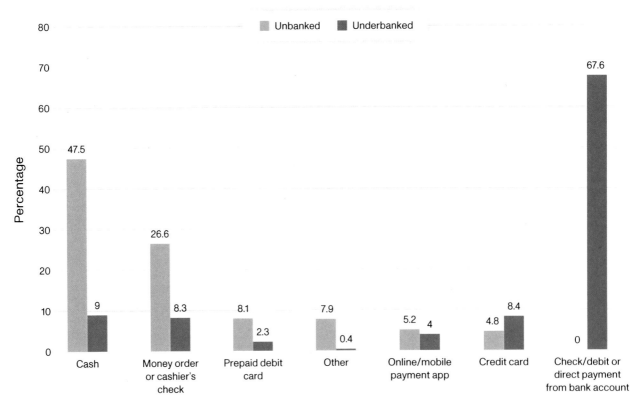

SOURCE: RAND California Survey of Household Finance (*n* = 344 unbanked households; *n* = 683 underbanked households).

Figure 2.7 | Method Most Often Used to Receive Money from Various Sources, by Banked Status

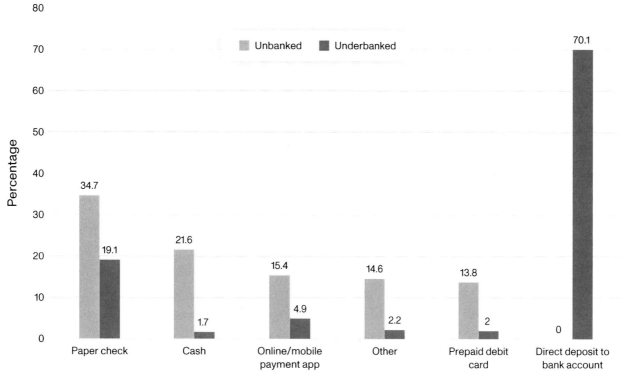

SOURCE: RAND California Survey of Household Finance (*n* = 344 unbanked households; *n* = 683 underbanked households).

Figure 2.8 | Method Most Often Used to Send Money to Family and Friends, by Banked Status

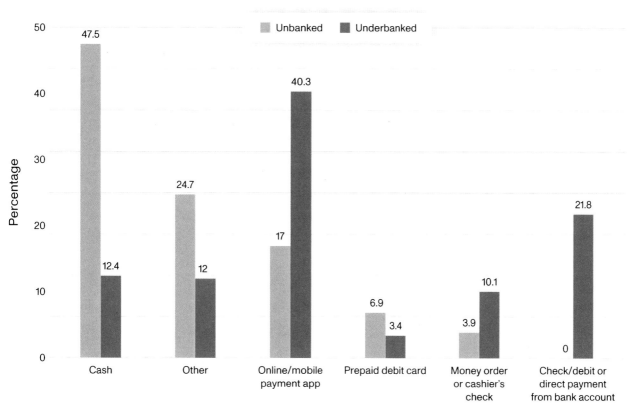

SOURCE: RAND California Survey of Household Finance (*n* = 326 unbanked households; *n* = 663 underbanked households).

Figure 2.9 | Method Most Often Used to Make In-Person and Online Purchases, by Banked Status

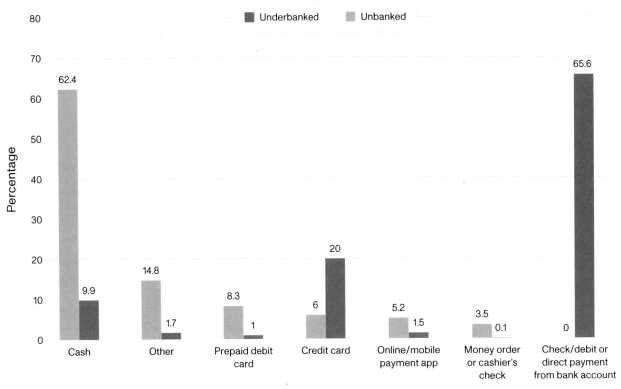

SOURCE: RAND California Survey of Household Finance (*n* = 344 unbanked households; *n* = 684 underbanked households).

Use of Online or Mobile Payment Services

Figure 2.10 illustrates a notable reliance on online or mobile payment services among households in the RAND survey sample, particularly among underbanked households. (*Online banking* refers to accessing bank services "using a computer or tablet"; *mobile banking* refers to accessing bank services "using an app, text messaging, or internet browser on a mobile phone."[11]) When we break this down by service provider, we see that all providers saw higher usage rates among underbanked households, with Apple Pay being the most popular among this group. Among unbanked households, Cash App was most popular.

As shown in Figure 2.11, both underbanked and unbanked households said that they predominantly use online or mobile payment services to send money to family or friends or to make purchases. Notably, a higher percentage of unbanked households said that they use these services to pay monthly bills than underbanked households, suggesting that, for the unbanked, these platforms may serve as an alternative to traditional banking for essential financial activities.

Overall, the survey results underscore the importance of online and mobile payment services as financial tools, with distinct patterns of usage and preferences between the two groups of households. These findings highlight the potential for online and mobile payments services to bridge some, but not all, gaps in traditional banking access.

Figure 2.10 | Use of Online or Mobile Payment Services, by Banked Status

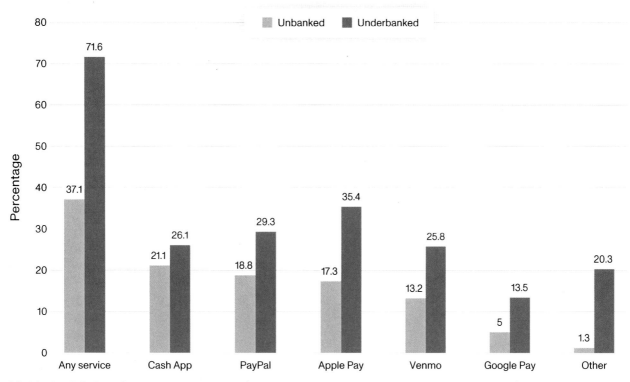

SOURCE: RAND California Survey of Household Finance (*n* = 348 unbanked households; *n* = 685 underbanked households).

Figure 2.11 | Financial Transactions Made Using Online or Mobile Payment Services, by Banked Status

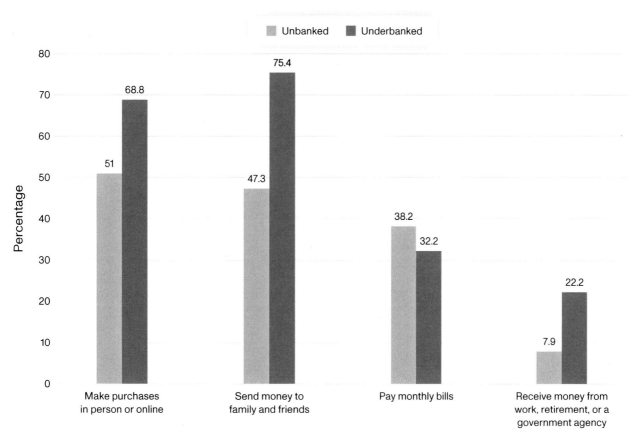

SOURCE: RAND California Survey of Household Finance (*n* = 127 unbanked households that report using online or mobile payment services; *n* = 462 underbanked households that report using online or mobile payment services).

Trust in Institutions and Financial Services

We examined the extent to which potential CalAccount participants place trust in institutions and financial services to provide further insight into the trust issue cited in Figure 2.5. Storing one's financial resources with a public or private external entity requires a substantial degree of trust on the part of the owner. If trust in a particular entity is low, it may be challenging to convince new customers to place their financial resources at risk. This may be especially so for populations in economically precarious situations, such as the unbanked. To explore the prevalence of trust, we analyzed responses to a question in which both unbanked and underbanked sample members were given a list of institutions and financial services and then asked whether they agreed or disagreed with the statement: "I trust [name of institution or financial service]."

As shown in Figure 2.12, trust in government and financial institutions, such as traditional banks, was relatively high, particularly among underbanked households. Interestingly,

the number of unbanked households that reported lacking trust in traditional banks does not correspond equally to the number of unbanked household who cited lack of trust as a reason for not having a bank account. More than two-thirds of both unbanked and underbanked households reported having trust in money transfer services. By contrast, fewer than half of unbanked and underbanked households said that they trust in payday loan/advance stores and pawn shops.

There was considerably more trust in online payment services among underbanked households than among unbanked households, which is perhaps unsurprising given their respective use of such services. With the exception of pawn shops, underbanked households place more trust in the list of institutions and financial services presented to them in the survey than do unbanked households. Of particular concern is how trust in the California government, the entity that would oversee CalAccount, compares with the others. Among the underbanked, levels of trust in banks (75.7 percent) and money transfer services (74.7 percent) were somewhat higher than levels of trust in the California

Figure 2.12 | Trust in Institutions and Financial Services, by Banked Status

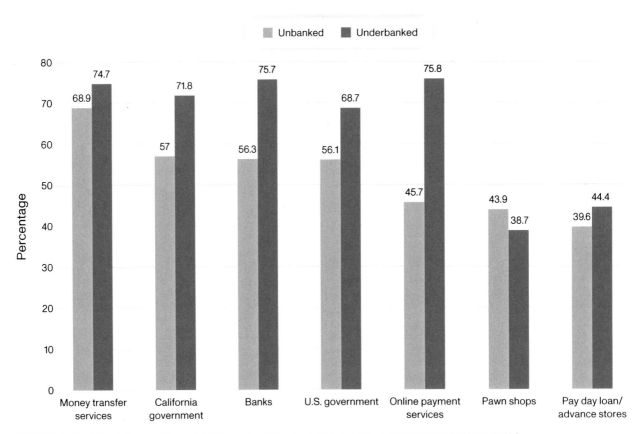

SOURCE: RAND California Survey of Household Finance (*n* = 342 unbanked households; *n* = 684 underbanked households).

government (71.8%). Because the underbanked already have bank accounts, by definition, and because they reported trusting banks more than they trust the California government, they might be unwilling to transfer their accounts to the CalAccount Program. Among the unbanked, levels of trust in the California government (57.0 percent) were on par with their trust in banks (56.3 percent). However, of all the institutions and financial service presented to them in the survey, the unbanked placed the most trust in money transfer services: 68.9 percent of unbanked California households in the RAND survey sample agreed with the statement "I trust money transfer services."

Figure 2.13 | Interest in Having a Bank Account Among the Unbanked

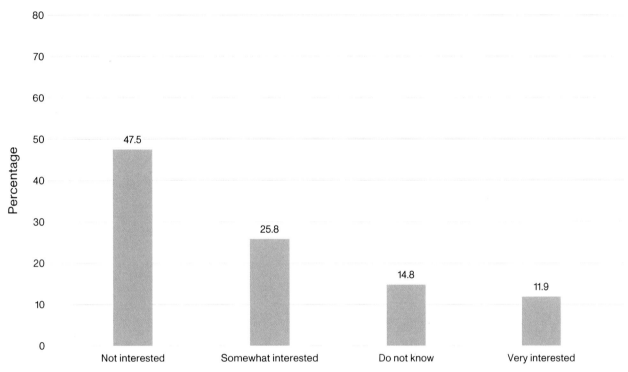

SOURCE: RAND California Survey of Household Finance (*n* = 346 unbanked households).

Likelihood of Opening a Bank Account

CalAccount's success as a sustainable state-run program is contingent in large part on the target population's decision to enroll. As shown in Figure 2.13, overall interest within the current banking landscape was low, with about one in ten unbanked households reporting that they were "very interested" in having a bank account, an additional quarter reporting that they were "somewhat interested," and a further 14 percent reporting that they didn't know. Just under half of unbanked households, the largest contingency, said that they were "not interested" in having a bank account.

The survey responses in Figure 2.13 reflect interest in having a bank account within the current status quo of the existing banking landscape in California. To further explore the likelihood that California residents might enroll in the CalAccount Program, we presented hypothetical scenarios with different account features to both unbanked and underbanked households (Figure 2.14; see the figure note for details).

As shown in Figure 2.14, the two features most likely to increase the likelihood of the unbanked and underbanked opening an account were a lack of minimum balance and a physical location at a bank. A majority of the underbanked and a plurality of the unbanked reported that with these two features, they would likely consider opening an account. Across the board, however, underbanked households were considerably more likely than unbanked households to open a new account regardless of the scenario presented. Moreover, there was no scenario under which the majority of unbanked households would likely open a bank account.

Taken together, Figures 2.12, 2.13, and 2.14 suggest that the group most in need of a bank account—the unbanked—might be difficult to persuade to enroll in CalAccount.

Figure 2.14 | Interest in Opening a Bank Account Under Different Scenarios, by Banked Status

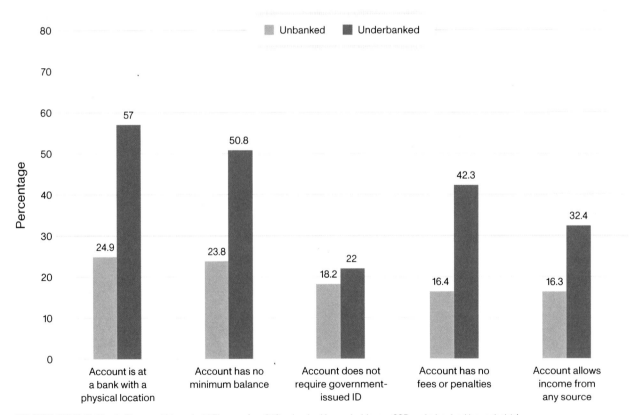

SOURCE: RAND California Survey of Household Finance (*n* = 346 unbanked households; *n* = 685 underbanked households).

NOTE: Unbanked households in the RAND survey sample were asked: "If you were offered the opportunity to open a checking or savings account, what features might convince you to take advantage of this opportunity?" The language was modified slightly for the underbanked, given that they already have a bank account. These households were asked: "'We understand that you currently have a checking or savings account. However, if you were offered the opportunity to open a new checking or savings account at a different bank, what features might convince you to take advantage of this opportunity in place of your current bank or credit union?'"

NOTES

[1] Bank branch locations were obtained from the Federal Financial Institutions Examination Council (FFIEC), "NIC National Information Center," database, undated-c (data accessed on January 29, 2024). Credit union branch locations were obtained from NCUA, "Call Report Quarterly Data," database, March 12, 2024b (using data from September 2023). The population count for each demographic group was obtained from the 2020 Decennial Census block-level data (via Esri Demographics Team, "California Census 2020 Redistricting Blocks," ArcGIS interactive map, accessed April 4, 2024). For a given locale, percentages represent the share of either the total population or a particular demographic group that resides more than x miles from the nearest branch office. Resident locations are approximated by the center points of U.S. Census blocks.

[2] Emily DiVito, *Banking for the People: Lessons from California on the Failures of the Banking Status Quo*, Roosevelt Institute, September 2022.

[3] Throughout our market analysis, we analyze the distribution of fees *charged* by the traditional banks, and later nonbanks, which is different from distribution of fees *paid* by the median customer, a value that is not observable through public datasets.

[4] Overdraft and NSF fees are generally levied on a per-transaction basis and are generally independent of the size of transactions or the amount by which the customer's account balance falls below zero (Trevor Bakker, Nicole Kelly, Jesse Leary, and Éva Nagypál, "Data Point: Checking Account Overdraft," Consumer Financial Protection Bureau, July 2014).

[5] The Consumer Financial Protection Bureau recently proposed to cap the overdraft fees that financial institutions with more than $10 billion in assets can charge. If implemented, the allowable overdraft fee would be capped at $3–$14 depending on which benchmark the CFPB would implement, which is lower than the current overdraft fee charged by 90 percent of the banks in California. See CFPB, "CFPB Proposes Rule to Close Bank Overdraft Loophole That Costs Americans Billions Each Year in Junk Fees," January 17, 2024).

[6] Dennis F. Campbell, Asís Martínez-Jerez, and Peter Tufano, "Bouncing Out of the Banking System: An Empirical Analysis of Involuntary Bank Account Closures," *Journal of Banking & Finance*, Vol. 36, No. 4, April 2012.

[7] Several financial institutions also offer check-cashing and money order services to nonrelationship clients. As an example, Bank of America charges $8 per check for amounts that exceed $50, and Chase Bank charges $5 per money order for amounts up to $1,000.

[8] FDIC, *2021 FDIC National Survey of Unbanked and Underbanked Households*, 2021a.

[9] One difference of note between the FDIC survey sample and the RAND survey sample is that the RAND survey sample includes substantially more individuals classified as having an "other" race. This is most likely because the FDIC does not have an explicit option for "other" race, although respondents do have the option to write in their race. The RAND survey includes an explicit option for "other" race.

[10] Jose Ivan Rodriguez-Sanchez, "An Economic Lifeline? How Remittances from the US Impact Mexico's Economy," Rice University's Baker Institute for Public Policy, November 13, 2023.

[11] FDIC, 2021a.

chapter
3

Feasibility Review of Key CalAccount Components

This chapter discusses the feasibility of the key components of CalAccount that are described in the California Public Banking Option Act—including the proposed nine-member CalAccount board, required account features, and enrollment of individuals who lack a federal or state government-issued photo ID and individuals without permanent housing. We also discuss feasibility challenges not directly related to these key components. We then provide recommendations for overcoming feasibility challenges.

We performed three key research activities to conduct this feasibility review:

- **Document review:** To develop a comprehensive understanding of policy, current business practices, and market dynamics relevant to CalAccount operations, we reviewed approximately 136 documents—including regulations, research literature, industry reports, and news publications—concerning best practices and potential challenges to evaluate the feasibility and merit of CalAccount and to develop associated recommendations for the program. We also conducted a review of legal literature concerning

barriers and challenges to implementation stemming from legal liabilities; fraud, theft, and abuse; privacy laws; advertising laws; the Community Reinvestment Act; and liability for discrimination.

- **Stakeholder discussions:** We held confidential, semistructured discussions with 42 individuals from 32 organizations, representing a variety of perspectives, including those from the banking industry and financial service providers, those with legal or regulatory expertise, those with knowledge about CalAccount customer needs, and banking and consumer finance researchers. The discussions were led by a RAND facilitator who tailored discussion questions to each participant's role and expertise.

- **Analysis of stakeholder discussions:** We developed a data-driven framework to analyze the notes from all 42 stakeholder discussions. This analytical framework involved identifying key themes, tagging relevant insights in the text, and analyzing the results for patterns. The findings from this analysis were used to inform the overall assessment of CalAccount feasibility and to develop associated recommendations.

BOARD STRUCTURE REQUIREMENTS

The California Public Banking Option Act calls for CalAccount to be overseen by a nine-member board consisting of private-sector and public-sector members, as follows:

- "(i) The Treasurer or the Treasurer's designee.

- (ii) The Commissioner of the Department of Financial Protection and Innovation [DFPI] or that person's designee.

- (iii) An individual with banking expertise, particularly expertise in transaction accounts and debit cards, appointed by the Senate Committee on Rules.

- (iv) An individual with expertise in economic and racial justice and cultural competence appointed by the Speaker of the Assembly.

- (v) An employee representative appointed by the Governor.

- (vi) An individual with expertise in banking or consumer financial services affiliated with an academic institution appointed by the Governor.

- (vii) An individual with banking expertise appointed by the Governor.

- (viii) A public banking advocate appointed by the Senate Committee on Rules.

- (ix) A consumer representative or advocate with expertise in banking access and financial empowerment, including within historically unbanked and underbanked communities, appointed by the Speaker of the Assembly."

The California Public Banking Option Act also details the duties of the board, which include

- developing a process for individuals to open CalAccounts to maximize participation

- creating no-fee options for depositing funds, including electronic transfers, and cash loading via partners

- setting up a process for direct deposit of earnings into CalAccounts

- establishing requirements for employers to deposit elected contributions into CalAccounts

- implementing no-fee withdrawal options using CalAccount debit cards, including ATMs and point-of-sale

- developing a process for no-fee payments to registered payees via electronic transfers

- defining conditions and processes for becoming a registered payee to encourage electronic payments and limit fees

- creating voluntary rules for automated payments based on account conditions

- facilitating account opening for individuals without ID, permanent housing, or minors

- selecting and overseeing an administrator to manage enrollment, direct deposits, and integration with other programs

- contracting with an administrator to manage financial services, issue secure debit cards, and maintain a fee-free transaction network

- developing and annually reevaluating a financial structure to ensure program sustainability.

The nine-member board size was universally well received in interviews, with one interviewee noting that the odd number of members prevents stalemates.

Regarding board composition, interviewees' responses generally reflected categories of members already contemplated in the legislation:

- "You've got to have bankers on there. Maybe draw from the legislature, [from] appropriate committees. Have some community-based organizations: people who actually serve CalAccount users."

- "You need someone with banking knowledge, FinTech knowledge, in that industry or been there." (See Box 1 on the next page.)

- "Community leaders should be involved in governance . . . consumer advocates should be involved, ones who work on these issues so they understand issues on the ground. Someone from a consumer-facing government department like DFPI, plus banking . . ."

Interviewees identified several existing oversight bodies that could be used as models for the CalAccount board:

- The nine-member CalSavers Retirement Savings Board governs California's retirement savings plan, focusing on "the results that the organization intends to achieve, not on the day-to-day management of the organization."[1] The board is authorized to make and enter into contracts, determine the duties of the program administrator, procure insurance against loss, and other activities associated with administration of the trust.[2] It is also responsible for reporting annually to the Legislature and governor.[3]

- The seven-member ScholarShare Investment Board governs the Golden State Scholarshare College Savings Trust and the California Kids Investment and Development Savings Program (CalKIDS). The board is similar to the CalSavers Retirement Savings Board with respect to composition, duties, and powers.[4]

- The 13-member Connecticut Green Bank Board of Directors oversees the operations of the quasi-governmental Connecticut Green Bank and is responsible for ensuring that the bank meets its goals and objectives related to supporting clean energy investments and environmental infrastructure in Connecticut.[5]

- The Bank of North Dakota (BND) is operated, managed, and controlled by the North Dakota Industrial Commission, which consists of three members: North Dakota's governor, agriculture commissioner, and attorney general. The governor appoints members "knowledgeable in banking and finance" to a seven-member BND Advisory Board. The Industrial Commission defines the advisory board's duties, including reviewing BND operations and making recommendations "concerning management, services, policies and procedures." Additionally, the

BND is subject to audit by the North Dakota Department of Financial Institutions.[6]

Interviewees questioned about the feasibility of a CalAccount board expressed little to no concern. The consensus among interviewees was that the California State Treasurer's Office is already equipped to effectively manage a board and that there are many models of successful boards to draw from. Nonetheless, interviewees offered recommendations concerning board membership and function:

- Clarify that the role of the board is to focus on the strategy and the long-term vision of the program and avoid bogging the board down in implementation.

- Ensure that the board has a clear understanding of the program's goals and expected benefits.

- Provide training and resources to the board to ensure that they have the necessary expertise to oversee the program effectively.

- Encourage open communication and collaboration among board members to ensure that the program is being overseen effectively.

27

Box 1. FinTech

FinTech, short for *financial technology*, represents a fusion of financial services and such contemporary technologies as application programming interfaces, cloud computing, biometrics, and artificial intelligence. FinTech innovations range from web- or mobile-based consumer interfaces to automated insurance underwriting and programmable digital currencies. Although FinTech is not specific to the California banking landscape, we include a brief discussion of digital deposits and payments because of their relevance to CalAccount.

Digital banking and digital payments are two key FinTech activities. Several types of business engage in these activities, including traditional banks, large technology firms, and relatively young technology-focused FinTech companies. *Digital banking* refers to banking activities enabled through FinTech mobile apps and online platforms rather than physical branches. Digital banks often involve a partnership between a consumer-facing FinTech and an FDIC-insured bank, as well as arrangements with ATM networks and retailers to provide limited in-person services. *Digital payments* allow individuals and businesses to use nonbank providers, such as Venmo and PayPal, to make electronic payments via services and products such as peer-to-peer payments and digital wallets. Some digital payment balances, such as those added through direct deposit, may be eligible for FDIC pass-through insurance. FDIC pass-through insurance covers funds held in deposit accounts at a FinTech company's partner bank, up to FDIC limits.

Digital banks tend to target specific market segments, often tech-savvy consumers with relatively simple banking needs. In contrast, digital payment firms tend to target a broader market, catering to consumers and businesses seeking convenient and fast online and mobile payment options.

A FinTech company's comparative advantage is its data, computing, and consumer interface, which enables it to tailor products and improve customer experience in ways that traditional banks may find difficult.[a] Some FinTech companies, such as certain payment services, are not subject to the same regulatory oversight as banks. These comparative advantages may enable these companies to lower the costs of, and significantly expand access to, financial services.[b] However, some argue that FinTech has not delivered on this promise and may even widen existing disparities in banking.[c]

FinTech do not necessarily replace traditional banking services. Large banks retain advantages in terms of customer base and resources.[d] Still, some banks and FinTech companies see their unique advantages as opportunities to partner in providing new tools to improve efficiency, customer experience, and regulatory compliance.[e]

---

[a] René M. Stulz, "FinTech, BigTech, and the Future of Banks," *Journal of Applied Corporate Finance*, Vol. 31, No. 4, Winter 2022, pp. 87, 89.

[b] Thomas Philippon, "On Fintech and Financial Inclusion," BIS Working Papers, No. 841, February 2020.

[c] Adam J. Levitin, "The Financial Inclusion Trilemma," *Yale Journal on Regulation*, Vol. 41, No. 1, January 2024.

[d] Stulz, 2022.

[e] Sami Ben Naceur, Bertrand Candelon, Selim Elekdag, and Drilona Emrullahu, "Is FinTech Eating the Bank's Lunch?" IMF Working Papers, WP/23/239, November 2023; Board of Governors of the Federal Reserve System, *Community Bank Access to Innovation Through Partnerships*, October 2023d.

ACCOUNT FEATURES

According to the California Public Banking Option Act, CalAccount should

1. serve "individuals who may not have federal or state government-issued photo identification"[7] and "individuals who do not have permanent housing"[8]

2. offer a zero-fee, zero-penalty transaction account and related payment services at no cost to account holders[9]

3. offer federally insured transaction accounts[10]

4. "enable and streamline remittance of local, state, and federal benefit and public assistance payments and other disbursements to account holders who are entitled to those payments and who authorize those payments to be directly deposited by electronic fund transfer into a CalAccount"[11]

5. enable payroll direct deposit by requiring employers with more than 25 employees and hiring entities with more than 25 independent contractors to have and maintain a payroll direct deposit arrangement that enables voluntary worker participation in the program[12]

6. establish the process and terms and conditions for becoming a registered payee, which should include limiting the late payment fees and penalties that registered payees can impose on account holders who pay them using preauthorized electronic fund transfers from their CalAccounts[13]

7. require "a landlord or a landlord's agent to allow a tenant to pay rent and deposit of security by an electronic funds transfer from a CalAccount."[14]

To gauge the feasibility of these features, we conducted a search for transaction accounts with these features through literature review and stakeholder interview. Our literature review and stakeholder interviews also explored potential obstacles that these account features may pose. The second column in Table 3.1 provides one or more examples of an already existing transaction account for each of the seven CalAccount features listed above. (These examples are further detailed in Box 2.) The third column summarizes feasibility concerns related to each feature.

In short, all the primary CalAccount features (with the exception of requiring registered payees to limit late fees) are features that are similar or identical to transaction account features already being offered through Bank On-certified banks, MoCaFi/Sunrise Banks, N.A., and other banks. (See Box 2 for a discussion of alternative accounts similar to CalAccount.) Nonetheless, despite the fact that these features are technically feasible, profitability and legal liability concerns on the part of banks and trust issues on the part of consumers may pose feasibility challenges, as further detailed in the "Other Obstacles" section later in this chapter.

Enrollment of Individuals Without a Photo ID and Individuals Who Lack Permanent Housing

The California Public Banking Option Act notes that CalAccount is intended to serve "individuals who may not have federal or state government-issued photo identification" and "individuals who do not have permanent housing."[15] The Bank Secrecy Act (BSA), a federal law that requires financial institutions to assist the U.S. government in detecting and preventing money laundering, requires banks to adopt a customer identification program (CIP) as part of their Know Your Customer (KYC) obligations.[16] At a minimum, per federal law, the procedures for opening an account must include collection of (1) name, (2) date of birth for an individual, (3) address (see section below on individuals who do not have permanent housing), and (4) ID number (taxpayer ID number for "U.S people," other options for "non-U.S. people").[17] A person, including a bank employee, who willfully violates the BSA or its implementing regulations is subject to a criminal fine of up to $250,000, five years in prison, or both.[18] An SME whom we interviewed noted that, in practice, some financial institutions contract with third-party KYC services, such as Socure or IDology.[19]

Table 3.1 | Account Features, Examples, and Feasibility Concerns

Feature	Examples	Feasibility Concerns
1. Individuals who lack state or federal picture ID, are unhoused, or are ages 14–18 can enroll	• One of Bank On's (see Box 2) strongly recommended features is accepting alternative IDs.[a] For example, banks that participate in San Francisco's Bank On initiative accept any valid passport (foreign or domestic) with photo; consular IDs from Argentina, Colombia, Dominican Republic, Guatemala, and Mexico; Documento Unico de Identidad (El Salvador); U.S. non-immigrant visa and border crossing card with photo; tribal ID; and/or San Francisco City ID.[b] • Chase Bank accepts Matricula Consular Card, passport with photo, student ID with photo, and U.S. Employment Authorization Card with photo.[c] • U.S. Bank's website notes: "We accept the Matricula Consular Mexicana as principal form of ID at all U.S. Bank branches."[d] • The MoCaFi Financial Services mobile account and debit card offered through Sunrise Banks, N.A. (hereinafter, "MoCaFi account"), accepts foreign IDs.[e]	**No major feasibility concerns.** Although individuals with no IDs will face challenges opening a bank account, individuals who lack a state or federal picture ID may prove their identity through alternative forms of identification. As further detailed below, many financial institutions already accept alternative IDs, such as municipal IDs, student IDs, and consular IDs.
2. Zero-fee, zero-penalty	• Bank On core (i.e., required) features include no opening/activation fee ($25 minimum deposit), no dormancy/inactivity fee, no account closer fee, no low balance fee, no overdraft fee, no monthly statement fee, and no customer service fee. However, Bank On–certified accounts are permitted to charge a monthly maintenance fee ($5 or less if not waivable, $10 or less if waivable – e.g., direct deposit).[f] • The MoCaFi account has no-fee cash withdrawals at Allpoint, Wells Fargo, and Citi ATMs; no-fee cash depositing on the VanillaDirect Network, including Rite-Aid, Walgreens, Dollar General, and Family Dollar; no-fee Mobile check load (for immediate fund) through Ingo Money (third-party service provider); and no overdraft features.	Offering low- and no-fee accounts at scale may not be profitable from a bank's perspective, and thus **banks may have little incentive to promote these accounts** (see discussion in "Other Obstacles" section later in this chapter).
3. Federally insured	• A Bank On core feature is that accounts be insured by the FDIC, the National Credit Union Share Insurance Fund, or a regulator-sanctioned equivalent. • The MoCaFi account is FDIC insured. (Sunrise Banks, N.A., is a member of the FDIC.) • Virtually all California state banks and national banks are insured by the FDIC.[g]	**No major feasibility concerns.**
4. Connectivity with other state and local government programs	• Most traditional banks, credit unions, and general-purpose reloadable prepaid cards provide a routing and account number for receiving government benefit funds into the account through direct deposit.[h] • However, government-issued prepaid cards, such as the Electronic Benefits Transfer (EBT) card, do not allow depositing funds from sources other than the government entity.	**No major feasibility concerns**, but fraud issues related to the California Employment Development Department unemployment benefits debit card and the EBT card highlight the importance of investment in fraud prevention technologies and processes.[i]

Table 3.1 | *continued*

Feature	Examples	Feasibility Concerns
5. Payroll direct deposit	• Most traditional banks, credit unions, and general-purpose reloadable prepaid cards provide a routing and account number for payroll direct deposit. Payroll direct deposit by employers is not currently required. However, a somewhat similar employer mandate is required under the CalSavers Retirement Savings Program, "which is an automatic payroll deduction retirement savings program for private sector employees in California who lack access to a workplace retirement plan" (see the "Employer Direct Deposit" section in Appendix B: CalAccount Legal Issues).[j]	**No major feasibility concerns**, particularly given the CalSavers precedent and popularity of direct deposit among employers. However, enforcement mechanisms would need to be developed. (See the "Employer Direct Deposit" section in Appendix B: CalAccount Legal Issues for legal analysis of employer mandates.)
6. Registered payees	• We did not locate any precedents for limitation of late fees that registered payees may charge individuals who have a specific type of bank account.	From a practical standpoint, **utility companies and other entities may choose not to register as payees because of the late fee limitation**. (See the "Limiting the Late Payment Fees and Penalties that Registered Payees Can Impose" section in Appendix B: CalAccount Legal Issues.)
7. Electronic funds transfer for deposits and rent	• We did not locate any precedents for requiring landlords to accept rent and deposit of security by an electronic funds transfer from a specific type of bank account. However, California laws reflect a general intent to allow tenants to pay rent via a method of their choosing.[k]	**No major feasibility concerns.**

[a] Several banks and credit unions in California offer Bank On–certified accounts, such as Bank of America SafeBalance Banking, Golden 1 Credit Union Easy Checking, and Provident Bank Teen Checking (Bank On, "Certified Accounts," webpage, undated-b). See Box 2.

[b] City and County of San Francisco, Office of Financial Empowerment, "Open a BankOn Account," webpage, undated.

[c] JPMorgan Chase, "How to Open a Bank Account for Non-U.S. Residents," webpage, undated.

[d] U.S. Bank, "Matrícula Consular Mexicana," webpage, undated.

[e] MoCaFi Mobility Account Agreement on file with authors.

[f] Cities for Financial Empowerment Fund, "Bank On National Account Standards (2023–2024)," fact sheet, undated-c.

[g] DFPI, "The Dual Chartering System and the Benefits of the State Charter," webpage, undated.

[h] General-purpose reloadable prepaid cards can be purchased at many major retailers, online, or directly from financial institutions. Users can add funds to the card via a bank transfer, direct deposit of paychecks and government benefits, cash deposit at approved retailers or the financial institution that provided the card, a mobile check load feature (if offered), or "reload pack" by purchasing from the retailers. See Contra Costa County Employment and Human Services, "Electronic Benefits Transfer (EBT)," webpage, undated.

[i] Lauren Hepler, "How EDD and Bank of America Make Millions on California Unemployment," CalMatters, February 5, 2021b; Jeanne Kuang, "California Missed Chances to Stop EBT Theft. It's Lost Tens of Millions of Taxpayer Dollars Since," CalMatters, November 8, 2023.

[j] California State Treasurer's Office, "California Secure Choice Retirement Savings Investment Board: Summary of Senate Bill 1234," October 24, 2016.

[k] California Civil Code, Division 3, Obligations, Chapter 2, Hiring of Real Property, Section 1947.3(a)(a), 2011, states that "a landlord or a landlord's agent shall allow a tenant to pay rent and deposit of security by at least one form of payment that is neither cash nor electronic funds transfer." AB 2219 (codified as an amendment to California Civil Code, Section 1947.3) requires a landlord or landlord's agent to allow a tenant to pay rent through a third party.

Box 2. Examples of Alternative Accounts Similar to CalAccount

Available to All Banks

Bank On

The Governor of California—with the support of financial institutions, city mayors, community-based organizations, and federal banking regulators—launched Bank On California in 2008. Bank On aims to provide consumers with low-fee bank accounts and build trust in the banking system through partnerships with community-based organizations.

In 2015, the Cities for Financial Empowerment Fund (CFE Fund), a financial empowerment–focused nonprofit organization, established nationwide benchmarks for Bank On affordable checking accounts. In crafting the benchmarks (e.g., no overdraft fees, robust debit card and online bill pay capabilities), the CFE Fund drew inspiration from the FDIC's Model Safe Accounts Template. The California Department of Financial Protection and Innovation (DFPI); then called the Department of Business and Oversight) took over responsibility for the statewide Bank On program in January 2016. The 2021 DFPI Bank On report noted: "Since the initial program launch in 2008, the Bank On California program has largely gone dormant due to lack of funding and collaboration with financial institutions."

As of May 2024, there are four active regional programs in California and 56 accounts offered by banks in the state that are Bank On–certified. A 2024 article in the *Yale Journal on Regulation* highlighted high closure rates among Bank On accounts nationally and posited that, given the average reported revenue and likely costs of maintaining these accounts, the accounts are not profitable to banks.[a] The article suggests that banks offer Bank On accounts despite low profitability to integrate unbanked customers for potential cross-selling, to gain Community Reinvestment Act credit, and to earn positive publicity and regulatory goodwill. According to the article, these benefits may incentivize financial institutions to offer Bank On accounts only on a limited scale. Individuals we interviewed for this market analysis also hypothesized that banks do not promote their Bank On–certified accounts because they are not profitable.

FinTech Collaborations with FDIC-Insured Financial Institutions

Angeleno Connect/MoCaFi

In April 2020, the City of Los Angeles launched the Angeleno Connect initiative to swiftly disburse pandemic-relief and poverty-alleviation funds. The Immediate Response Incentive Card, a fee-free banking service introduced with this initiative, provides easy access to monetary transfers and other benefits for unbanked and other eligible Angelenos. Starting in October 2020, in collaboration with financial services company MoCaFi, the city expanded the functionality of the initial card to allow Angelenos to deposit money, expanding financial services for many who are unbanked or underbanked. In December 2022, MoCaFi started issuing cards solely to enhance the number of Angelenos with access to banking services. The original contract with MoCaFi and its extensions have concluded, so the city is currently evaluating new funding and contracting options. Angeleno Connect received over 450,000 applications and assigned almost 38,000 cards to households, directly benefiting 105,000 individuals.

The Angeleno Connect Card and associated banking services were supported by partnerships with Mastercard's City Possible™ platform, IGNITE Cities, and Wells Fargo Bank.

Middle Class Tax Refund Card

The California Middle Class Tax Refund (MCTR) was proposed by Governor Gavin Newsom and approved by the Legislature as a one-time payment to help qualified Californians who filed a 2020 tax return respond to higher costs caused by inflation. The program, which provided $9.5 billion to California families, distributed the refund via a prepaid debit card to individuals who mailed in their return or did not have direct deposit set up with the Franchise Tax Board. The MCTR Card allowed users to make purchases at stores accepting Visa debit cards and get cash at ATMs, banks and credit unions, and participating stores.

SOURCES: California Department of Financial Protection and Innovation, *BankOn California*, 2021; CFE Fund, "About Bank On," webpage, undated-c; Bank On Coalition, *Playbook: Equipping Bank On Coalitions for Local Banking Access Success*, California Department of Financial Protection and Innovation, 2021; Bank On, "100 Coalitions," webpage, undated-a; CFE Fund, "Bank On National Account Standards (2023–2024)," fact sheet, undated-c; interviews with Participants 102 and 110.

[a] Levitin, 2024.

There is no one-size-fits-all solution to verifying identity without state and federal IDs.

Federal Regulations Explicitly Discuss Nondocumentary Methods of Identity Verification

Federal regulations require banks to include a description of how banks verify the identity of customers, including "when the bank will use documents, non-documentary methods, or a combination of both methods."[20]

With respect to nondocumentary procedures, the regulations state the following:

- "These methods may include contacting a customer; independently verifying the customer's identity through the comparison of information provided by the customer with information obtained from a consumer reporting agency, public database, or other source; checking references with other financial institutions; and obtaining a financial statement"

- "The bank's non-documentary procedures must address situations where an individual is unable to present an unexpired government-issued identification document that bears a photograph or similar safeguard."[21]

Official Guidance Explicitly Discusses Ways to Verify Identity Without State or Federally Issued ID

With respect to documentary methods, the FDIC notes: "A bank that accepts items that are considered secondary forms of ID, such as **utility bills and college ID cards**, is encouraged to review more than a single document to ensure that it has formed a 'reasonable belief' of the customer's true identity" (emphasis added).[22] In its official guidance, the NCUA notes that other forms of ID, including an **employee ID card**, "may be used if they enable the bank to form a reasonable belief that it knows the true identity of the customer," but cautions that, "given the availability of counterfeit and fraudulently obtained documents, a bank is encouraged to obtain more than a single document to ensure

that it has a reasonable belief that it knows the customer's true identity."[23]

With respect to nondocumentary methods, the FDIC also notes that "in instances when an account is opened over the Internet, a bank may be able to obtain an **electronic credential**, such as a digital certificate, as one of the methods it uses to verify a customer's identity" (emphasis added).[24]

On its website, the Consumer Financial Protection Bureau (CFPB) addresses the question of whether individuals can get bank accounts without a driver's license:

> Banks and credit unions are required to verify your identity when you apply to open an account. . . . The most common way to verify your identity is with a driver's license. There are other ways banks and credit unions can verify your identity, so if you don't have a driver's license, ask the bank or credit union what types of identification it will accept. **The rules leave some discretion to banks and credit unions on what forms of ID to accept.** (emphasis added)[25]

Regulations and Official Guidance Highlight Risk-Based Approach and Institutional Discretion

There is no one-size-fits-all solution to verifying identity without state and federal IDs in the CIP context. As noted above, federal regulations require banks to adopt a CIP "based on the bank's assessment of the relevant risks"[26] and official guidance by federal regulators states that banks can accept non-government-issued ID "if they enable the bank to form a reasonable belief that it knows the true identity of the customer."[27] In addition, the FDIC provides the following guidance on verifying customer identity information:

> The CIP should rely on a risk-focused approach when developing procedures for verifying the identity of each customer to the extent reasonable and practicable. **A bank need not establish the accuracy of every element of identifying information obtained in the account opening process, but must do so for enough information to form a "reasonable belief" that it knows the true identity of each customer.** At a minimum, the risk-focused procedures must be based on, but not limited to, the following factors:

33

i. Risks presented by the various types of accounts offered by the bank;

ii. Various methods of opening accounts provided by the bank;

iii. Various sources and types of identifying information available; and

iv. The bank's size, location, and customer base. (emphasis added)[28]

Some Financial Institutions in California Accept Alternative Forms of ID to Open Bank Accounts

As of the time of this writing in early 2024, the City and County of San Francisco's Office of Financial Empowerment website notes that some financial institutions that participate in San Francisco's Bank On initiative accept any valid passport (foreign or domestic) with photo; consular IDs from Argentina, Colombia, the Dominican Republic, Guatemala, and Mexico; Documento Unico de Identidad (El Salvador); U.S. non-immigrant visa and border crossing card with photo; tribal ID; and/or San Francisco City ID.[29] (Each San Francisco Bank On participating financial institution determines what IDs it will accept—i.e., participants do not have an agreed-upon list of alternative IDs. The list presented here is a combination of IDs accepted by different financial institutions.) Notably, an SME we interviewed for this study mentioned that the CFE Fund cites alternative IDs (e.g., municipal IDs, consular IDs) as "strongly recommended features" for financial institutions that participate in Bank On, but does not include a requirement that financial institutions accept any specific types of alternative IDs as a core Bank On feature because ID requirements are governed by federal regulations.[30]

Chase Bank maintains a webpage titled "How to open a U.S. bank account for non-residents," which notes that the following are acceptable forms of ID: Matricula Consular Card, passport with photo, student ID with photo, and U.S. Employment Authorization Card with photo.[31] U.S. Bank's website notes: "We accept the Matricula Consular Mexicana as principal form of ID at all U.S. Bank branches."[32]

Individuals Who Lack Permanent Housing Can Still Meet the Regulatory Address Requirement

According to federal CIP regulations, for an individual, banks need to obtain "a residential or business street address, or if the individual does not have such an address, an Army

Post Office (APO) or Fleet Post Office (FPO) box number, or the residential or business street address of next of kin or of another contact individual."[33] Guidance provided by the Board of Governors of the Federal Reserve System, the FDIC, the Financial Crimes Enforcement Network, NCUA, the Office of the Comptroller of the Currency, the Office of Thrift Supervision, and the U.S. Department of the Treasury notes that, for purposes of compliance with this requirement, the number on the roadside mailbox on a rural route, a residential or business address for next of kin or another contact individual, or a description of a customer's physical location will suffice.[34] In the context of veterans experiencing homelessness who wish to open a bank account, the U.S. Department of Veterans Affairs (VA) notes that "a VA Homeless Coordinator's office address can be used in place of a home address when the account holder has a valid VA ID and does not have a permanent address to provide to the financial institution. A financial institution can accept the residential or business address of another contact individual, such as the aforementioned VA Homeless Coordinator."[35]

In short, regulations and official guidance afford discretion to financial institutions to verify accountholder identity, but financial institutions are responsible for weighing the risk of accepting nongovernmental identification. In addition, banks incur financial costs associated with verifying customer identities. **We conclude, therefore, that there is no one-size-fits-all solution to CIP requirements, but there are already alternative methods (apart from state and federal IDs) for complying with CIP requirements.** To best serve potential CalAccount participants who do not have state or federal IDs, CalAccount should select partner financial institutions that are able to meet CIP regulatory requirements while still accepting alternative forms of ID. In addition, outreach to CalAccount holders and unbanked Californians generally should highlight the alternative forms of ID that financial institutions accept; the availability of a California state ID for undocumented individuals;[36] and the availability of municipal IDs for those unbanked individuals in municipalities such as San Francisco,[37] Richmond,[38] and Oakland.[39] Appendix B contains a more detailed description and analysis of KYC requirements.

34

OTHER OBSTACLES

Aversion to Perceived Legal Liability Risks May Affect Bank Participation in CalAccount

Two of our interviewees who work in the banking sector noted that fear of legal liabilities on the part of banks is likely to pose a significant barrier to financial institution partnership.[40] For example, these interviewees mentioned BSA and KYC rules and regulations; liability for fraud, theft, and abuse; privacy laws; advertising laws; unfair business practices laws; and liability for discrimination as areas likely to be of concern for financial institutions considering partnering with the state on CalAccount.[41] (See the "Legal Liabilities" section in Appendix B for discussion of potential legal liabilities.) Though some interviewees suggested that banks that offer CalAccount should be exempted from certain regulations or indemnified against legal liability,[42] the State of California cannot exempt banks from federal banking regulations, and the state is not generally permitted to indemnify parties with which it contracts.[43] In addition, shielding banks from liability could result in undesirable incentives (e.g., if a bank did not face potential fines and damage payments, the bank could be disincentivized from adopting robust anti-fraud measures).

Lack of Profitability May Disincentivize Banks from Offering or Promoting CalAccount

Several interviewees, including banking sector interviewees, expressed doubt that CalAccount could be profitable, with some specifically noting that interchange fees would be unlikely to offset the costs of opening and maintaining accounts.[44] Interviewees also noted that if CalAccount is not profitable, banks would be reluctant to promote it.[45] Some of these interviewees indicated that Bank On–certified accounts are not well promoted for this reason. As discussed in Box 2, the Bank On California program has reportedly largely gone dormant, in part because of lack of collaboration with financial institutions.[46] A 2024 article in the *Yale Journal on Regulation* postulated that Bank On accounts' lack of profitability has incentivized banks to offer these accounts on only a small scale.[47] Nonetheless, as detailed in Chapter 4 of this report, depending on how CalAccount is structured, the program could become revenue-neutral within 10 years. In addition, as further detailed in the "Strategies for Overcom-

ing Obstacles" section below, community-based organizations (CBOs) and government agencies could provide the outreach and promotion that banks may not be incentivized to undertake.

Lack of Trust in Banks May Pose Barrier to Uptake by Unbanked and Underbanked Individuals

Some interviewees reported that unbanked and underbanked Californians lack trust in banks because of historical discrimination and/or because they felt unwelcome or dismissed during past interactions with financial institution staff.[48] Interviewees also suggested that people who primarily communicate in languages other than English may not trust banks because lack of communication fosters suspicion and uncertainty about banking practices.[49] In addition, interviewees noted that individuals may have concerns about how information they provide to banks is being shared with such government agencies as U.S. Immigration and Customs Enforcement.[50] Another concern that interviewees expressed was that money deposited into bank accounts could have tax implications, be seized to satisfy debts or legal judgments, or lead to disqualification from government benefits programs.[51]

Interviewees stressed the importance of extensively researched and tailored outreach and engagement efforts.

STRATEGIES FOR OVERCOMING OBSTACLES

Interviewees suggested strategies for overcoming potential lack of CalAccount promotion on the part of banks and lack of trust on the part of potential CalAccount holders. Interviewees did not provide recommendations for overcoming potential lack of profitability. Although some interviewees mentioned indemnification as a way to address banks' concerns about legal liabilities, as noted above, the state is generally not permitted to indemnify parties with which it contracts and indemnification could lead to undesirable incentives.

Partnerships with Community-Based Organizations and Government Agencies and Programs

Partnerships with CBOs and government agencies with deep knowledge of their clients' needs and modes of doing business could foster trust and improve uptake and use of CalAccount. In addition, collaborating with government and tribal agencies that offer social safety-net benefits and consumer protection services could also encourage participation among Californians who do not trust banks. CBOs and government agencies could help promote CalAccount to their clients through a number of channels, such as in person at the organization's office and during fairs and outreach events, on websites and social media, and via mailings and text messages.

In addition, assistance with enrollment, direct deposit of government benefits and labor income, and account management support could be offered through already-existing financial empowerment and tax assistance programs. For example, staff and volunteers at the Volunteer Income Tax Assistance Program,[52] city and county financial empower-

ment centers,[53] and libraries[54] could receive training to assist prospective and existing CalAccount holders.

Partnerships with CBOs and government and tribal agencies could also widen and deepen CalAccount's footprint and help target specific geographic areas as needed.[55] For areas without easy access to banks, CalAccount could consider innovative approaches, such as the "RV-based bank" run by a Bank On–certified credit union in Fresno that brings physical banking services to residents' doorsteps.[56]

User-Friendly, Culturally Appropriate Program Materials

Interviewees stressed the importance of extensively researched and tailored outreach and engagement efforts to specific market segments.[57] Outreach materials would explain how to enroll in CalAccount and the features and benefits of the program. Although general program messaging should be consistent, materials would also address specific needs, such as how to open an account without a state or federal picture ID. All materials would be available in multiple languages and incorporate cultural considerations (e.g., provide examples of alternative forms of ID that specific communities may have access to). These materials would be distributed to CBOs, as well as third parties, such as landlords and employers.

Program materials could also include a banking "bill of rights" that incorporates, for example, a plain-language explanation of state and federal privacy protections.[58] Such a document could also provide a plain-language explanation of what types of deposits cannot be taken from their bank accounts, even if the account holder owes someone money as part of a legal judgement against them.[59]

Processes for Gathering and Using Feedback to Improve CalAccount

To ensure that CalAccount continues to meet Californians' needs and to maintain trust with account holders, the program should develop processes for gathering feedback and using that feedback to improve CalAccount. One interviewee suggested implementing surveys, a hotline, or other mechanisms that allow customers to provide direct and immediate feedback as well as employing secret shoppers or canvassers for this purpose.[60]

NOTES

[1] California State Treasurer's Office, "California Secure Choice Retirement Savings Investment Board: Governance Policies," July 22, 2019. Board membership is defined in California Government Code, Title 21, The CalSavers Retirement Savings Trust Act, Section 100002.

[2] California Government Code, Title 21, Section 100010.

[3] California Government Code, Title 21, Section 100038.

[4] California Education Code, Title 3, Postsecondary Education; Division 5, General Provisions; Part 42, Student Financial Aid Program; Chapter 2, Student Financial Aid Programs; Article 19, Golden State Scholarshare Trust Act, Sections 69980–69994; California Education Code, Article 19.5, California Kids Investment and Development Savings Program, Sections 69996–69996.9.

[5] Connecticut Green Bank, "Governance," webpage, undated; General Statutes of Connecticut, Title 16, Public Service Companies; Chapter 283, Telephone, Gas, Power and Water Companies, Section 16-245n, Connecticut Green Bank, Charge Assessed Against Electric Customers, Clean Energy Fund, Environmental Infrastructure Fund.

[6] Bank of North Dakota, "History of BND," webpage, undated.

[7] Section 100104(a)(1)(K) of the California Public Banking Option Act (AB 1177) states, in part, that "the board, in establishing processes for enrollment in the CalAccount Program: (i) Shall facilitate the opening of a CalAccount by individuals who may not have federal or state government-issued photo identification while taking all reasonable steps to maintain the confidentiality of personal information consistent with all applicable law."

[8] Section 100104(a)(1)(K) of the California Public Banking Option Act (AB 1177) states, in part, that "the board, in establishing processes for enrollment in the CalAccount Program: … (ii) Shall design and establish rules governing the enrollment and participation in the program of individuals who do not have permanent housing."

[9] AB 1177, Section 100104(a)(1)(A).

[10] AB 1177, Section 100104(a)(1)(A).

[11] AB 1177, Section 100104(a)(1)(L)(v).

[12] AB 1177, Section 100104(a)(1)(O).

[13] AB 1177, Section 100104(a)(1)(I).

[14] AB 1177, Section 100104(a)(1)(P).

[15] AB 1177, Section 100104(a)(1)(K).

[16] U.S. Code, Title 31, Subtitle IV, Chapter 53, Subchapter II, Records and Reports on Monetary Instruments Transactions, Section 5311 *et seq.* See Office of the Comptroller of the Currency, "Bank Secrecy Act (BSA)," webpage, undated-a.

[17] Code of Federal Regulations, Title 31, Section 1020.220(a)(2)(i)(A). See also FDIC, "Bank Secrecy Act, Anti-Money Laundering, and Office of Foreign Assets Control," in *DSC Risk Management Manual of Examination Policies*, Section 8.1, December 2004; FFIEC, "BSA/AML Examination Manual: Introduction," webpage, undated-a. For "non-U.S. people," ID numbers may include "Customer's TIN, passport number and country of issuance, Alien ID card number, and number and country of issuance of any other (foreign) government-issued document evidencing nationality or residence and bearing a photograph or similar safeguard" (FDIC, "Bank Secrecy Act, Anti-Money Laundering, and Office of Foreign Assets Control," in *DSC Risk Management Manual of Examination Policies*, Section 8.1, December 2004). See also FFIEC, "Customer Identification Program," in *Bank Secrecy Act (BSA)/Anti-Money Laundering (AML) Examination Manual*, February 2021.

[18] U.S. Code, Title 31, Subtitle IV, Chapter 53, Subchapter II, Records and Reports on Monetary Instruments Transactions, Section 5322(a).

[19] Participants 121 and 122, interview with the authors. See also "Dibbs Taps Socure for 'Know Your Customer' Platform, Identity Verification," PYMNTS, April 5, 2022. There are many other providers of customer identity services, such as LexisNexus Risk Solutions (identified by Participant 101), which provides a suite of CIP services (LexisNexis, "Customer Identification Program," webpage, undated).

[20] Code of Federal Regulations, Title 31, Section 1020.220, note to paragraph (a)(2)(i)(A)(4)(ii).

[21] Code of Federal Regulations, Title 31, Section 1020.220(a)(2)(ii)(B).

[22] FDIC, 2004.

[23] National Credit Union Administration, "Interagency Interpretive Guidance on Customer Identification Program Requirements Under Section 326 of the USA PATRIOT Act," April 28, 2005.

[24] FDIC, 2004.

[25] Consumer Financial Protection Bureau, "Can I Get a Checking Account Without a Driver's License?" webpage, August 19, 2020.

[26] Code of Federal Regulations, Title 31, Section 1020.220(a)(2).

[27] NCUA, "FAQs: Final CIP Rule," RA2004-04Encl, 2004.

[28] FDIC, 2004, p. 8.1-10. See also FFIEC, 2021.

[29] City and County of San Francisco, Office of Financial Empowerment, undated.

[30] Participant 112, interview with the authors. Bank On "core features" and "strongly recommended features" are listed in CFE Fund, "Bank On National Account Standards (2021–2022)," webpage, undated-b.

[31] JPMorgan Chase, undated.

[32] U.S. Bank, undated.

[33] Code of Federal Regulations, Title 31, Section 1020.220(a)(2)(i)(A)(3).

[34] Financial Crimes Enforcement Network, "Interagency Interpretive Guidance on Customer Identification Program Requirements Under Section 326 of the USA PATRIOT Act," U.S. Department of the Treasury, April 28, 2005.

[35] Veterans Benefits Administration, "Opening an Account at a Financial Institution for Veterans Without Permanent Housing," fact sheet, U.S. Department of Veterans Affairs, undated.

[36] Office of Governor Gavin Newsom, "California IDs For All," September 23, 2022.

[37] City and County of San Francisco, "Get a Free SF City ID Card," webpage, May 15, 2023.

[38] City of Richmond, "Richmond Municipal Identification/Stored Value Card," webpage, undated.

[39] City of Oakland, "General Information - Información General, Oakland City Identity Card," webpage, undated.

[40] Participants 108 and 109, interview with the authors.

41 Participants 108 and 109, interview with the authors.

42 Participants 108, 109, and 110, interview with the authors.

43 California Department of General Services, *California State Contracting Manual*, Vol. 1, June 2023, Chapter 7, Section 7.86.

44 Participants 102, 110, 117, 118, 119, 120, and 127, interview with the authors.

45 Participants 102, 110, 117, 119, and 120, interview with the authors.

46 DFPI, "Organizing a State Credit Union: Information Booklet," DFPI-391, Rev. 09-2023, September 2023.

47 Levitin, 2024.

48 Participants 104, 107, 116, 118, 119, 120, 128, 129, 133, and 134, interview with the authors.

49 Participants 104, 107, 116, 118, 119, 120, 128, 129, 133, and 134, interview with the authors.

50 Participant 111, interview with the authors.

51 Participant 135, interview with the authors. Asked about sequestration, the interviewee named child support and tax liens as examples.

52 California State Controller's Office, "Volunteer Income Tax Assistance (VITA) Program," webpage, undated.

53 See, for example, Los Angeles County, "Center for Financial Empowerment," webpage, undated; City and County of San Francisco, Office of Financial Empowerment, undated.

54 See, for example, Ventura County Library, "Financial Empowerment Class," webpage, undated; Berkeley Public Library, "Personal Finance at the Library, Appointments," webpage, March 23, 2021.

55 Participant 113, interview with the authors.

56 Participant 106, interview with the authors.

57 Participants 111 and 131, interview with the authors.

58 Participants 111 and 132, interview with the authors.

59 See Judicial Branch of California, "Collect Money from a Bank Account, California Courts Self-Help Guide, undated; Judicial Council of California, "Exemptions from the Enforcement of Judgments," EJ-155, September 1, 2021.

60 Participant 129, interview with the authors.

chapter
4

Options for CalAccount

We modeled various policy options for CalAccount to evaluate the relative cost-effectiveness of potential banking structures the program might take. These policy options are not specific proposals for CalAccount, and they do not endorse specific choices for the Commission. Instead, in lieu of final details on the structure and implementation of CalAccount, the policy options we describe are hypothetical scenarios intended to reflect the scope and magnitude of potential social and economic impacts (i.e., benefits, costs, and transfers) of CalAccount under different sets of assumptions regarding the general structure of the program.

We modeled three policy alternatives for CalAccount (see Table 4.1) that differ in terms of the scope of the financial network. Specifically, the policy options vary by mode of access, which include mobile banking, ATMs, and bank or credit union branches, as well other options for in-person banking. Differences in the available modes of access have implications for the projected enrollment rates, with enrollment rates increasing along with the size of the financial

Table 4.1 | Potential Policy Options for CalAccount

	Option 1: Mobile Banking	Option 2: Mobile Banking + Existing Brick-and-Mortar Financial Network	Option 3: Mobile Banking + Expanded Brick-and-Mortar Financial Network
Expected enrollments	Low	High	Highest
Size of financial network	Access to a robust and geographically expansive ATM network, with limited or no access to in-person banking	Access to a robust and geographically expansive ATM network, including bank or credit union branches	Access to a robust and geographically expansive ATM network, including bank or credit union branches plus additional state-designated locations

41

network. In addition, we modeled different levels of program awareness and subsequent enrollment. This reflects the resources (e.g., financial and person-hours) dedicated to maximizing program enrollment via community outreach, advertising, and other public messaging strategies. Other policy decisions may specify administrative measures to operate the program. For example, additional implementation options for the Commission may include identifying and selecting partner financial institutions, FinTech companies, hardware and software providers, and/or web-based or application developers. At this stage, these decisions are outside the scope of the feasibility study and do not inform the estimation of economic impacts.

Within each of the three policy options, we consider low-end, midpoint, and high-end enrollment scenarios. The enrollment estimates are a combination of the scope of the financial network, the disposition toward opening a CalAccount (see Appendix D for full details), and the proportion of the population who become aware of CalAccount, presumably through outreach efforts or other information channels. Within each scenario, the main driver of differences in enrollment numbers is variation in the proportion of the unbanked and underbanked who become aware of the CalAccount Program. Specifically, we bound the percentage of unbanked and underbanked households that become aware of program between 25 and 75 percent, with 25 percent being a low-awareness outcome and 75 percent being a high-awareness outcome.[1]

We develop a BCA framed around these three policy options. BCAs provide a useful framework to evaluate and compare investments or policy decisions. Specifically, they measure improvements in economic efficiency resulting from a policy or program or the net change in overall societal welfare. For this study, the BCA is intended to provide a rough-order-of-magnitude assessment of the potential social and economic impacts of possible CalAccount options. It is important to note that the analysis relies on a number of assumptions that could vary significantly from the actual implementation plan for the program.

BENEFIT-COST ANALYSIS

Our BCA identifies and describes the benefits and costs of each policy option for different groups of stakeholders, including state agencies, businesses, and individuals. We also estimated secondary macroeconomic impacts, including impacts on jobs in California. To the extent feasible, we quantify these impacts in monetized dollar terms to allow decisionmakers to evaluate different policy options using a common measure. Where it is not feasible to monetize potential program benefits, we provide qualitative evidence of impacts. We note that, as a general rule, some important benefits and costs may be difficult to quantify or monetize. In particular, it can be challenging to monetize impacts associated with a public good that provides benefits that are intangible and difficult to measure, such as financial stability, quality of life, or equity. When it is not possible to

monetize all the important benefits and costs, policymakers should consider all the evidence available to determine how important the nonmonetized benefits may be in the context of the overall analysis, as the policy with the largest monetized net benefits may not be the policy that most improves social welfare.[2]

We estimate the potential impacts of the CalAccount Program over the first 10 years after its implementation. This time horizon is intended to be sufficient to capture benefits that may accrue to stakeholders over several years (in comparison to program costs that are more likely to be incurred on an upfront basis) and answer questions about the ability of the program's benefits to "break even" or offset those costs over time.[3]

To compare benefits and costs that accrue in different time periods, we discount all future impacts using a standard rate. The U.S. Office of Management and Budget (OMB) recommends that federal agencies discount future benefits and costs to reflect the social rate of time preference (also referred to as "the time value of money") using a discount rate of 2 percent.[4] This value reflects the real rate of return on long-term U.S. government debt (on a pre-tax basis) over a 30-year period between 1993 and 2022. The rate of return on private capital may differ from the social rate of time preference, and therefore different industries may have different time preferences. For example, OMB previously found that the average rate of return to capital was approximately 7 percent as estimated in 1992 and recommended that agencies use this value as a base case discount rate. For this study, we rely on the most-recent guidance, recommending a 2 percent discount rate.[5]

Benefits and Costs Evaluated

Benefits

We consider both monetized and nonmonetized benefits to individuals and businesses. For CalAccount's primary target population—the unbanked and underbanked—the immediate impacts of access to a checking account include an insured mechanism for storing money, direct deposit options for tax refunds and paychecks (if offered by employer), and access to a robust and geographically expansive network of participating ATMs to access cash. Longer-term benefits for the unbanked and underbanked include a reduced need to use costly transactional alternative financial services and new household savings. The estimated benefits to institu-

> **CalAccount's benefits for the unbanked and underbanked include a reduced need to use costly transactional alternative financial services.**

tions administering the program include increased revenues through return on deposits on new accounts and interchange fees associated with increased debit card use.

With respect to state agencies, there are additional potential efficiency gains that could result from establishing CalAccount. First and foremost, there is an opportunity to roll the administrative features of other state benefit programs into the CalAccount Program. Beneficiaries could receive electronic funds transfer of state benefits directly deposited into a CalAccount, potentially saving the state the costs of mailing checks or issuing prepaid debit cards separately for each state program. This could also consolidate various program oversight functions into a single state agency or office for a greater cost savings to the state.

Costs

The estimated costs in our analysis represent the total burden on the economy and include both up-front, one-time costs (e.g., capital expenditures) and recurring costs (e.g., operations and maintenance) associated with the program's implementation. The direct program costs include those incurred by individuals (e.g., the time it takes to enroll in the program), by financial institutions not participating in CalAccount (e.g., from loss of fees when underbanked customers transfer to CalAccount),[6] by alternative financial services (e.g., from reduced demand for check cashing and other services), by retailers (e.g., from fees associated with increased FinTech use), by landlords (e.g., from fees

43

associated with taking Automated Clearing House [ACH] payments), and employers (e.g., from costs associated with maintaining payroll direct deposit).

We also include the fiscal impacts to state agencies, such as the costs of establishing the CalAccount Program, possible fee structures and potential benefits for the state through the revenue-sharing arrangement with the financial services network administrator, and enforcement costs. We estimate program costs for the three policy options based on various assumptions about the fixed and variable costs of developing administrative policies and procedures, investing in financial technology, conducting enrollment and customer identity verification, staffing, and other costs.

Transfers

In addition to quantifying and monetizing the direct benefits and costs of different policy options for the CalAccount Program, our analysis evaluates transfers between affected groups. Generally, transfer payments result in a reallocation of money or resources from one group to another group.[7] In the case of CalAccount, there are several potential countervailing policy impacts, including (1) fees that individuals pay for alternative financial services that may be displaced by having access to direct deposit via CalAccount (i.e., a transfer from alternative financial services businesses to individuals), (2) fees that individuals pay associated with traditional bank accounts (e.g., overdraft fees) that may be displaced by having access to a no-fee account (i.e., a transfer of from financial institutions to individuals), and (3) monetary transfers from traditional bank accounts among the underbanked population into CalAccount (i.e., a transfer from one financial institution to another).

Table 4.2 summarizes the types of costs, benefits, and transfers associated with the different policy options, respectively.

Table 4.2 | Potential Costs, Benefits, and Transfers Associated with Policy Options for CalAccount

	Option 1: Mobile Banking	Option 2: Mobile Banking + Existing Brick-and-Mortar Financial Network	Option 3: Mobile Banking + Expanded Brick-and-Mortar Financial Network
Potential costs	• Outreach • Enrollment • Account maintenance • Issuing debit cards • Customer service • Direct deposit service	Option 1 costs *plus* • ATM hardware and software • Interface with state systems	Option 2 costs *plus* • Identifying and assessing new markets/customer segments • Monitoring and evaluating impact • Lease/construction • Office equipment/furniture • Staffing and training to support expanded financial network
Potential benefits	• Increased access to financial services • Safety of account holders • Accrued savings • Entrepreneurship • Building financial history • Potential revenue to banks through return-on-deposits and interchange fees	Option 1 benefits *plus* • Access to in-person banking options	Option 2 benefits *plus* • Access to enrollment options or other program support in certain state/local government buildings (or other locations)
Potential transfers	• Other fees (e.g., overdraft, check-cashing, payday loans) • Monetary transfers to CalAccounts		

FINDINGS FROM THE BENEFIT-COST ANALYSIS

Under the assumptions presented in this preliminary analysis, the overall societal benefits of CalAccount likely exceed its costs over a 10-year period, given sufficient program enrollment. The net benefits are estimated to be around $4 million or less on an annual basis and are negative under our low-end enrollment projections. However, not all of the benefits of the program can be monetized, and this estimate may understate the overall net benefit of the program. Nonmonetized benefits of the program include increased financial inclusion and financial literacy, improved household financial stability, enhanced health and public safety outcomes, and opportunities for financial innovation, such as increased adoption of financial technology and partnerships between financial institutions and community-based organizations.

The societal benefits of the program accrue primarily to unbanked and underbanked households in California, while participating financial institutions would benefit from increased revenue from new deposits and interchange fees due to increased debit card use and the state may benefit from a revenue-sharing agreement with the financial services network administrator. The primary impact of the program would be a significant income transfer from traditional financial institutions and alternative financial services to unbanked and underbanked households in California. Specifically, the avoidance of fees would reduce industry profits while boosting household disposable income. We estimate that unbanked and underbanked households, on average, would avoid fees for financial services totaling $70 to $150 per year. We also estimate that unbanked households would increase their overall level of household savings by approximately $450 to $1,200. This amount of savings could have a significant impact on the well-being of low-income households, easing the burden of financial insecurity and reducing the need for short-term lending in an emergency (e.g., a car repair or medical bill).

We find that the cost of operating the CalAccount Program may not be economically feasible for a financial services network administrator without a subsidy. Given the estimated average value of deposits in a CalAccount, the total estimated program revenues are less than $50 per account per year. Our review of various industry sources suggests that it costs banks, on average, between $175 and $400 per

Operating the CalAccount Program may not be economically feasible for a financial services network administrator without a subsidy.

year to maintain a customer account. For the state, under the assumptions presented in the BCA, there are potential revenue-sharing arrangements that could make the program revenue-neutral with regard to operating costs within 5 to 10 years—however, the state would likely not recoup the significant outreach costs to reach a sustainable level of enrollment. While transfers from other financial institutions to CalAccount and decreased demand for alternative financial services would likely result in job losses in the financial services sector (estimated between 150 and 200 jobs, in perpetuity), the program would likely result in job gains across other sectors of the economy (estimated between 350 and 500 jobs, in perpetuity).

Using a traditional benefit-cost framework, which seeks to maximize economic efficiency, Option 2 provides the greatest net societal benefits. This reflects that under Option 1 (the mobile banking option), enrollment would potentially be limited by lack of access to high-speed internet, lack of trust in financial technology, or a preference to bank at a physical branch location. Furthermore, although Option 3 provides the greatest total benefits, it yields the smallest net benefit because increased access to banking services comes at a cost of staffing alternative banking options in nontraditional locations (e.g., post offices) that would exceed the monetized benefits associated with households that would be unlikely to enroll otherwise (e.g., those for whom the distance to the nearest branch was a significant barrier to banking, such as those in banking deserts).

Table 4.3 reports the midpoint enrollment estimate (i.e., the average of the low- and high-end awareness estimates) of the benefits and costs for each of the policy options described in this study. As shown, the costs are generally higher in the first two years of the program, which reflects the costs of developing a website, mobile app, new banking policies and procedures, enrollment, and outreach. However, the permanent loss of fee revenue from closed accounts and ongoing operations and maintenance costs associated with the program indicate that costs will be spread across several years. Benefits will also accrue over multiple years—these include avoided fees, which are calculated on an ongoing annual basis, and a one-time increase in household savings, which is estimated to occur within two years after the initial enrollment with a one-year lag. Note that initial enrollments are estimated to be evenly split across the first two years of the program. Once an account holder has built a new precautionary level of savings (i.e., the new steady state), no additional savings impacts are estimated. Benefits decline slightly over time because there are fewer projected new enrollments each subsequent year.

As noted, the feasibility of the CalAccount Program is highly dependent on enrollment. Figure 4.1 provides a sensitivity analysis across the three policy options using the low-end, midpoint, and high-end enrollment estimates presented in this report. Since many of the program's costs are fixed and its benefits are variable, under the low-enrollment projections we predict that the costs of the program will exceed its benefits and that the program will produce a negative return on investment. For the midpoint and high-end enrollment estimates, we estimate that the program's benefits over its first 10 years will exceed the costs, producing a positive social return on investment. This finding highlights the importance of marketing and outreach, because enrollment will depend on generating awareness of the program.

Table 4.3 | Summary of Benefits and Costs by Year Using a 2% Discount Rate ($2023, millions)

Year	Option 1			Option 2			Option 3		
	Benefits	Costs	Net Benefits	Benefits	Costs	Net Benefits	Benefits	Costs	Net Benefits
1	49.3	101.8	−52.4	59.0	120.1	−61.1	66.0	134.0	−68.0
2	134.5	148.4	−13.9	159.7	171.4	−11.6	176.8	190.9	−14.1
3	169.3	98.8	70.5	200.3	118.7	81.6	220.3	135.9	84.5
4	132.7	98.9	33.8	157.6	118.7	38.9	174.4	135.8	38.6
5	96.6	98.0	−1.4	115.5	117.6	−2.1	129.1	134.5	−5.4
6	95.8	97.1	−1.3	114.6	116.6	−2.0	128.0	133.2	−5.2
7	95.0	96.1	−1.1	113.6	115.4	−1.8	126.9	131.9	−5.0
8	94.1	95.2	−1.2	112.5	114.3	−1.8	125.7	130.5	−4.9
9	93.2	94.3	−1.1	111.4	113.2	−1.8	124.5	129.2	−4.7
10	92.3	93.3	−1.0	110.3	112.0	−1.6	123.3	127.8	−4.6
10-year PV	1,053	1,022	30.9	1,254	1,218	36.6	1,395	1,384	11.2
Annualized value	114.9	111.5	3.4	136.9	132.9	4.0	152.2	151.0	1.2

NOTE: PV = present value. The 10-year PV is the sum of the discounted stream of benefits or costs. The annualized value, which represents the average annual impact taking into account the discount rate, is calculated as the present value divided by the sum of discount factors.

Figure 4.1 | Projected 10-Year Net Present Value, by Policy Option and Enrollment Level

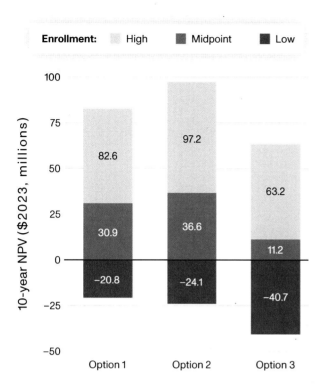

Enrollment: ▢ High ■ Midpoint ■ Low

10-year NPV ($2023, millions)

Option 1: 82.6 (High), 30.9 (Midpoint), −20.8 (Low)
Option 2: 97.2 (High), 36.6 (Midpoint), −24.1 (Low)
Option 3: 63.2 (High), 11.2 (Midpoint), −40.7 (Low)

NOTE: NPV = net present value. The 10-year PV is the sum of the discounted stream of benefits and costs.

Figure 4.2 displays our estimates of the program's net present value (NPV) by group across each of the three policy options. While the values vary by policy option, the results show that the greatest benefits are accrued by unbanked and underbanked households participating in CalAccount—the monetized benefits (midpoint estimates) total between approximately $1.0 billion and $1.4 billion, depending on the policy option. The participating financial institutions also accrue benefits from revenue generated by banking services (i.e., revenue from deposits and interchange fees on debit card transactions). However, the NPV of costs for participating banks are projected to exceed their benefits. That is, the costs of establishing a CalAccount Program, enrolling individuals, and covering operating expenses are likely to exceed the average revenues from those accounts. The figure also shows costs incurred by alternative financial service providers due to a loss of business, costs incurred by merchants from increased transaction costs, and costs incurred by the State of California from administering the program.[8]

Given the significance of distributional impacts associated with the proposed CalAccount Program, we conducted a supplemental analysis applying distributional weights that reflect estimates of society's preferences for the overall distribution of income to the BCA presented above. Using distributional weights is intended to allocate investments to where they provide the greatest impact on social well-being, rather than where they maximize economic efficiency or provide the greatest return on investment. This provides another point of reference to make informed policy decisions. OMB guidance states that "agencies may choose to conduct a benefit-cost analysis that applies weights to the benefits and costs accruing to different groups in order to account for the diminishing marginal utility of goods when aggregating those benefits and costs."[9]

We apply utility weights of 7.1 and 3.2 to all benefits and costs for the unbanked and underbanked, respectively, and 1.0 for all other groups.[10] Given the relatively lower median income of the unbanked and underbanked relative to other California households, the choice of weights is notably large. Using these values, we recalculate the results for the "weighted" BCA. Whereas the unweighted BCA showed a negative net benefit for the low-end estimate, the weighted BCA shows a positive net benefit. Therefore, policymakers might decide that the net welfare gain of financial inclusion for the unbanked and underbanked using the

47

Figure 4.2 | Projected Annualized Benefits and Costs, by Group and Policy Option ($ 2023, millions)

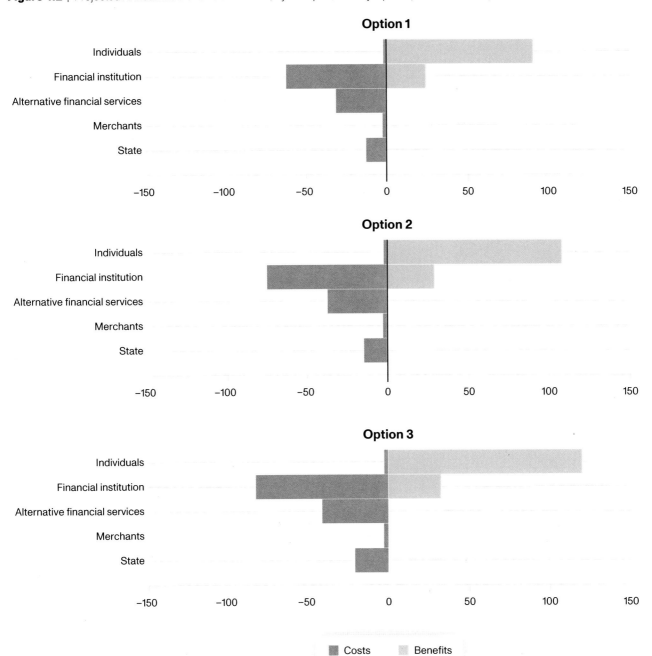

distributional weights outweighs the risk of a net social loss in the unweighted benefit-cost analysis under the low-end enrollment projections.[11] Furthermore, using distributional weights changes the ranking of policy options. In the weighted BCA, Option 3 (mobile banking plus an expanded brick-and-mortar financial network) yields the greatest net social benefit as opposed to Option 2 in the unweighted BCA. This suggests that using distributional weights to inform policy decisions would prioritize increasing enrollment over

the relative cost-effectiveness of the CalAccount Program in order to maximize societal well-being. Table 4.4 reports the midpoint estimates using distributional weights for each of the policy options.

Potential Household Savings from CalAccount Participation

In this section, we estimate the savings from no longer needing to use certain alternative financial services and from reduced fees among participants in the CalAccount by demographics.

One of the significant benefits for California households that elect to participate in the CalAccount Program are the potential savings from avoiding fees associated with banking and the use of alternative financial services. We estimate these potential savings, by demographic group, by estimating the accumulated savings from avoided fees associated with nonbank check cashing, nonbank money orders, prepaid

Table 4.4 | Projected Annualized Benefits and Costs, by Group ($2023, millions)

Year	Option 1			Option 2			Option 3		
	Benefits	Costs	Net Benefits	Benefits	Costs	Net Benefits	Benefits	Costs	Net Benefits
1	153.9	125.7	28.2	183.5	148.5	34.9	204.2	165.5	38.7
2	564.0	172.0	391.9	665.4	199.5	465.8	729.3	222.2	507.1
3	810.4	99.1	711.3	952.3	118.9	833.4	1,037.8	136.2	901.6
4	549.3	99.1	450.2	648.1	119.0	529.0	710.3	136.2	574.2
5	294.0	98.2	195.8	350.6	117.9	232.7	390.1	134.8	255.3
6	290.8	97.3	193.5	346.7	116.8	229.8	385.7	133.5	252.2
7	287.2	96.3	190.9	342.4	115.6	226.7	380.9	132.1	248.9
8	282.9	95.4	187.5	337.3	114.5	222.8	375.3	130.7	244.5
9	278.9	94.4	184.5	332.5	113.3	219.2	369.9	129.3	240.6
10	275.0	93.4	181.7	327.9	112.1	215.8	364.8	127.9	236.9
10-year PV	3,786	1,071	2,715	4,486	1,276	3,210	4,948	1,448	3,500
Annualized value	413.2	116.9	296.4	489.7	139.3	350.4	540.1	158.1	382.0

NOTE: The 10-year PV is the sum of the discounted stream of benefits or costs. The annualized value, which represents the average annual impact taking into account the discount rate, is calculated as the present value divided by the sum of discount factors.

cards, overdraft fees, account maintenance fees, and ATMs.

We exclude some potential costs, including international remittances and credit products, from this analysis, because those costs that may endure. In Appendix C, we provide detail on our estimations and specific assumptions used.

Table 4.5 shows estimates of savings in year 2027, or year two for CalAccount, when we estimate the program will have reached a steady state.[12] The table includes savings per household and total savings across households by demographic group. For example, we estimate that average savings to individual non-White unbanked households that participate in the CalAccount would be $62 and estimated savings to all non-White unbanked households that participate would be $10.5 million. Table 4.5 shows that the savings per unbanked household varies from $41 among households that are not low-income up to $101 among unmarried male households. Savings per underbanked household varies from $131 among unmarried male households up to $185 among non-Hispanic households.

Potential Impact on Disparities

Another impact of the CalAccount Program is its potential to reduce disparities in unbanked and underbanked rates, such as those discussed in Chapter 2.[13] Table 4.6 presents the disparity results for the three policy options and by high awareness (i.e., 75 percent of the unbanked and underbanked population know about the CalAccount Program) and low awareness (25 percent about the CalAccount Program).[14] The baseline disparities are in percentage points; for example, the unbanked rate for non-White households is 3.6 percentage points greater than the unbanked rate for White households. We show expected impacts in the rates of unbanked and underbanked Californians under the different CalAccount options and level of awareness as percentage changes. For example, the percentage change in the non-White vs. White household unbanked disparity is 9 percent under Option 1 with low awareness. This means that the 3.6 percentage point baseline disparity in unbanked rates fell by 9 percent to approximately 3.2 percentage points. Except for the underbanked disparity between unmarried households and married couples, there are (generally substantial) reductions

Table 4.5 | Estimated Savings to Unbanked and Underbanked Households Participating in CalAccount by Demographics, Option 2, High Enrollment, 2027

	Unbanked Households		Underbanked Households	
	Per-Household Savings	Total Household Savings (in $ millions)	Per-Household Savings	Total Household Savings (in $ millions)
Non-White households	62	10.5	148	88.9
White households	85	5.4	158	25.5
Non-Hispanic households	84	10.0	185	67.4
Hispanic households	61	7.1	156	61.6
Married households	37	3.3	140	49.7
Unmarried male households	101	6.2	131	24.5
Unmarried female households	79	5.8	171	39.7
Low-income households	87	11.5	172	37.9
Non-low-income households	41	4.2	164	87.0
Migrant households	72	1.2	133	6.9

SOURCE: Authors' analysis using data from the FDIC and RAND surveys.

NOTE: *Savings* refers to savings from avoided fees associated with nonbank check cashing, nonbank money order fees, prepaid card fees, overdraft fees, account maintenance fees, and ATM fees. Estimates assume the CalAccount Program has reached a steady state and that the CalAccount Program includes mobile banking and brick-and-mortar using an existing financial network with 75 percent of unbanked and underbanked households being aware of the CalAccount Program.

Table 4.6 | Impact of CalAccount on Disparities in Unbanked and Underbanked Rates

	Baseline Disparity	% Change in Disparity, Low Awareness			% Change in Disparity, High Awareness		
		Option 1	Option 2	Option 3	Option 1	Option 2	Option 3
Unbanked							
Race/Ethnicity							
Non-White vs. White households	3.6	−9.0%	−10.4%	−11.2%	−26.9%	−31.3%	−33.7%
Hispanic vs. non-Hispanic households	3.8	−10.1%	−11.8%	−12.7%	−30.4%	−35.5%	−38.1%
Household Structure							
Unmarried vs. married households	2.5	−5.7%	−6.6%	−7.1%	−17.0%	−19.8%	−21.3%
Unmarried female vs. unmarried male households	−1.4	−1.0%	−1.2%	−1.3%	−3.0%	−3.5%	−3.8%
Household Income							
Low-income vs. non-low-income households	12.5	−8.2%	−9.5%	−10.2%	−24.5%	−28.6%	−30.7%
Underbanked							
Race/Ethnicity							
Non-White vs. White households	12.6	−10.8%	−12.9%	−14.6%	−32.3%	−38.8%	−43.7%
Hispanic vs. non-Hispanic households	12.8	−10.8%	−13.0%	−14.6%	−32.5%	−38.9%	−43.7%
Household Structure							
Unmarried vs. married households	0.9	2.2%	2.6%	2.9%	6.6%	7.8%	8.8%
Unmarried female vs. unmarried male households	0.3	−4.6%	−5.7%	−6.6%	−13.9%	−17.1%	−19.7%
Household Income							
Low-income vs. non-low-income households	9.8	−8.3%	−9.9%	−11.1%	−24.8%	−29.7%	−33.4%

SOURCE: Authors' analysis using data from the ing data from the FDIC and RAND surveys.

NOTE: High awareness assumes that 75 percent of the unbanked and underbanked population know about the CalAccount Program, and low awareness assumes 25 percent of the unbanked and underbanked population know about the CalAccount Program. The samples are restricted to nonmigrant households.

in disparities from each of the CalAccount options considered, with the reduction in disparities being greatest in the high-awareness case for Option 3.

The disparity analysis, detailed in its entirety across Appendixes E and F, reveals that the CalAccount Program could have a sizable impact on reducing disparities in unbanked and underbanked rates for demographic groups of interest. In particular, we estimate that there could be large reductions in disparities between minority and nonminority groups, low-income and non-low-income households, and migrant and nonmigrant households. We also estimate large reductions in disparities in unbanked and underbanked rates between unmarried and married households, for which we note that baseline disparity includes a moderately higher rate of unbanked unmarried males than females and a moderately higher rate of underbanked unmarried females than males. Although these benefits are not directly quantifiable, they should be taken into consideration when evaluating the costs and benefits of CalAccount. However, CalAccount is not estimated to eliminate disparities in unbanked and underbanked rates in any scenario considered; at most, disparities are reduced by about 45 percent.

Potential Longer-Term Benefits

In addition to the direct monetized benefits of CalAccount, we examined several potential longer-term benefits of the program by reviewing various areas of the literature. Table 4.7 provides a high-level summary of our findings from the literature review; additional details and citations of sources are provided in Appendix F.

The findings in Table 4.7 are meant to provide examples of the types of outcomes that could be affected by participating in CalAccount and document approximate magnitudes of these impacts where possible. They are not meant to provide a comprehensive list of beneficial outcomes from the implementation of a CalAccount Program.

Table 4.7 | Outcomes That CalAccount Could Affect

Type of Outcome or Effect	Description of Potential Benefit
Financial outcomes	• Literature shows that economic stimulus payments affect savings, debt, and spending. • Literature shows that financial inclusion can promote wealth, savings, financial literacy, and trust in banks, as well as reduce financial insecurity. Studies also show that financial inclusion can help protect account holders from financial hardship during natural disasters and promote banking status of children. • Use of alternative financial services (AFS) is correlated with lower financial literacy. • Credit AFS has been documented to have negative impacts, but there are also harms associated with loss of access to credit AFS. Negative impacts include increased difficulty paying rent, mortgage, and utility bills; higher rates of public assistance usage; and higher rates of missed childcare payments. Research documents that loss of access to payday loans is correlated with higher likelihood of bank overdrafts and late bill payments and with deterioration in self-reported financial condition.
Health outcomes	• Studies link banked status to improved health and lower food insecurity. • Use of credit AFS has been linked with worse health outcomes.
Public safety outcomes	• While the literature generally suggests that more income reduces crime, the actual amount that individuals save when migrating from transaction-based AFS products to CalAccount is likely small compared with the programs and interventions studied in the literature. The highest-quality study in this literature shows no effect of housing vouchers on crime. • The literature on public safety and a lower demand for fringe banks remains largely correlational. Even if demand for such services as check cashing and money orders decreases, demand for credit-based services such as payday lending will likely remain unchanged. • There is some evidence suggesting that the availability and circulation of cash itself can affect local crime rates. CalAccount will likely reduce the amount of cash in circulation as users adopt debit cards and other banking services, such as direct deposit and electronic bill pay/money transfer.
Effects on FinTech	• Evidence suggests that the increased use of debit cards led small retailers (e.g., corner stores) to increase adoption of point-of-service (POS) systems. When program beneficiaries switched from using cash to debit cards, an indirect network externality was that more corner stores adopted POS systems—and, plausibly because of the added convenience, other (wealthier) consumers shifted 13 percent of their typical supermarket consumption to small retailers, whose sales and profits increased. Similar effects have been noted with adoption of mobile payment technologies.

Table 4.7 | *continued*

Type of Outcome or Effect	Description of Potential Benefit
Effects on banks[a]	• The literature shows that financial inclusion can promote wealth, savings, financial literacy, and trust in banks and increase the likelihood that children of newly banked individuals are banked in the future. SMEs suggested that the CalAccount Program could create financial stability for low-income participants and expand the long-term market for banks. • SMEs described the importance of leveraging CBOs and state agencies for outreach, which suggests that participating banks would form partnerships with these entities. • Multiple SMEs described how CalAccount would compete with banks that already provide banking options to low-income populations, including credit unions, community banks, and banks offering Bank On accounts. • Many SMEs expressed concerns about the risks and costs that banks would experience if they were to offer a CalAccount, with some noting how Bank On is not profitable, despite the ability to charge some fees for the account, and that the banks cover the costs of offering Bank On themselves. • In terms of benefits to banks, some SMEs said that offering a CalAccount would help banks improve their Community Reinvestment Act (CRA) ratings, conferring a variety of modest regulatory benefits. • Some SMEs mentioned that the CalAccount Program could improve the reputation of participating banks while others felt that there would be little to no impact.

NOTE: Appendix F provides details on the literature reviewed for this analysis, including citations of specific sources.

[a] Potential benefits to banks were developed through both a review of the literature and SME interviews with experts in the banking industry, legal and regulatory communities, organizations reflecting customer needs, and the academic and research communities that study banking and financial inclusion.

NOTES

1 Given limited information on what the desired level of outreach would be for CalAccount, we chose these percentages to provide a broad range for what awareness level might be achieved. See Appendix D for full details, including tables that allow for calculating how a change in the assumed awareness would affect estimated enrollment.

2 OMB, "Regulatory Analysis," Circular A-4, November 9, 2023.

3 This time horizon was selected in response to California Government Code, Title 21.1, CalAccount Blue Ribbon Commission, Section 100104(a)(3)(A), which requires the market analysis "include whether or not CalAccount Program revenue is more likely than not to be sufficient to pay for CalAccount Program costs within six years of the CalAccount Program's implementation."

4 OMB, 2023.

5 The results are not highly sensitive to the choice of discount rate because both benefits and costs are generally spread across several years with only some costs, such as website development, enrollment, and outreach costs, incurred primarily on an upfront basis.

6 We abstract away from the potential competitive effect on pricing in our analysis. Given high switching costs between banks and the presence of low- and no-fee banking products currently offered in California, we think this impact is likely low.

7 OMB, 2023.

8 Fumiko Hayashi, "Cash or Debit Cards? Payment Acceptance Costs for Merchants," *Economic Review*, Federal Reserve Bank of Kansas City, Vol. 106, No. 3, August 2021.

9 OMB, 2023.

10 Distributional weights are calculated using the following formula:

$$w_i = \left(\frac{\bar{y}_i}{y_{med}}\right)^{-\epsilon}$$

where $\bar{y}_i$ is the median household income of the specified subpopulation (i.e., the unbanked or under-banked); y_{med} is the median Californian household income; and ϵ is the absolute value of the elasticity of marginal utility. OMB recommends using a value of 1.4 for the elasticity of marginal utility. OMB recommends using a value of 1.4 for the elasticity of marginal utility.

11 A net social loss was calculated for the low-end estimates for all three policy options due to pessimistic enrollment projections. A net social gain was calculated for the midpoint and high-end estimates in the unweighted BCA.

12 The basis for assuming that CalAccount reaches steady-state enrollment within two years comes from Claire Célerier and Adrian Matray, "Bank-Branch Supply, Financial Inclusion, and Wealth Accumulation," *Review of Financial Studies*, Vol. 32, No. 12, December 2019. They show that U.S. interstate branching deregulation increased the probability of low-income households holding a bank account just one year after the policy took effect.

13 Detailed results from our disparity analysis are included in Appendix E with full descriptions of supporting methods included in Appendix F.

14 As previously noted and detailed in Appendix D, estimated enrollment numbers are a product of the scope of the financial network, the subjective likelihood of take-up of CalAccount by the unbanked and underbanked, and the level of awareness among the unbanked and underbanked. The estimated enrollment numbers vary the most by the low- vs high-awareness assumptions. We present results here split by the assumed level of awareness to provide a plausible range of estimates.

chapter

5

Check `n` Go

LOANS UP TO $255

GET CASH TODAY

ALL CHECKS CASHED

CASH ADVANCES

MONEY ORDERS AVAILA

STORE HOURS

Money Orders
099

PULL

PULL

This store protected by:
• Video surveillance • 10 minute time delay safe
• ADT hold up alarms

Esta sucursal se protege por:
• Vigilancia de video • Caja fuerte con retraso de
tiempo de 10 minutos • Alarmas ADT contra robo

Discussion and Conclusion

Through a survey of California's unbanked and underbanked populations, an analysis of the landscape of banking and nonbank alternatives across California, a review of key CalAccount components, and analyses of benefits, costs, and potential long-run impacts of the CalAccount Program, this report responds to the California Public Banking Option Act's request for a market analysis to determine whether it is feasible to implement the CalAccount Program.

In this concluding chapter, we provide a summary of our key findings and their associated trade-offs, discuss potential limitations associated with our analysis, and provide a set of recommendations.

THE FEASIBILITY OF PROPOSED CALACCOUNT OPERATIONS

The California Public Banking Option Act proposes that the CalAccount Program include several key features: a nine-member board with public- and private-sector membership; the ability to serve individuals who lack state or federal picture ID or are unhoused, and Californians ages 14–18; zero fees and zero penalties; federal deposit insurance; connectivity to state and local programs; payroll direct deposit; reg-

istered payees; and the ability for electronic funds transfers for deposits and rent payments. While our assessment finds no prohibitive concerns that would prevent the program's implementation, there are two notable areas where feasibility could be a concern.

Bank Incentives to Voluntarily Participate in CalAccount

First, CalAccount is only feasible if at least one FDIC-insured bank is willing to participate. Given that the decision of whether there will be one or multiple banks is ultimately a future decision to be made by the State of California, we consider both as options in our analysis. Our assessment, review of relevant literature, and interviews with SMEs suggest that offering no-fee accounts, at scale, may not be profitable and may not, on its own, provide ample incentive to banks to participate in CalAccount. Given the average value of deposits in a CalAccount, the total estimated CalAccount Program revenues are less than $50 per account per year. Our review of various industry sources suggest that it costs banks, on average, between $175 and $400 per year to maintain a customer account. Banks that charge monthly maintenance fees have a median fee of $7.88, or approximately $95 per account per year. The result is that

CalAccount Program revenues may not be sufficient to cover the basic costs of account maintenance. Additionally, interviews suggest that perceived legal liability risks related to KYC requirements and disparities in lending relative to deposit-taking activity may be a further barrier to bank participation.

However, our analysis also shows potential benefits for a bank that participates in the CalAccount Program. The program will generate revenue from interchange fees and through gains from fractional reserve lending. Table 5.1 lists CalAccount's projected revenues for the three policy options we examined. These funds could be available in a revenue-sharing agreement between the state and a partnering financial institution(s).

Beyond program revenues, the potential for building longer-term relationships with previously unbanked and underbanked customers may provide an additional incentive. For example, customers who become more comfortable and familiar with their CalAccount bank may open other accounts or consider traditional credit services (e.g., car loans or mortgages). Ultimately, banks' willingness to participate in the CalAccount Program may depend on their assessment of potential trade-offs between costs, risks, and the ability of state support to subsidize the customer acquisition costs to meet a sufficient enrollment number.

Reaching Sufficient Enrollment for Long-Term Sustainability

The second area where feasibility could be a concern is enrollment in the CalAccount Program. Enrollment is one of the most critical inputs to our analysis of the potential costs and benefits of the CalAccount Program.

The largest barrier to enrollment is lack of interest among California's unbanked and underbanked populations. As noted in Chapter 2, when asked about their interest in having a bank account, just over one in ten households in the RAND survey said they were "very interested," an additional quarter said they were "somewhat interested," and roughly 15 percent said they "don't know." Just under half said they were "not interested." Responses to other survey questions suggest that CalAccount features—including no fees, no minimums, and physical locations—may help increase interest. That said, our findings also revealed that trust will be a key barrier to overcome for CalAccount to succeed. Only somewhat more than half of unbanked Californians in our survey said that they trust either banks or the state government (56 and 57 percent, respectively); across interviews, we noted a similar theme regarding the likelihood that a lack of trust would pose a barrier to uptake. We return to the issue of trust in the discussion of key considerations later in this chapter.

Fundamentally, our assessment that benefits can marginally outweigh costs is dependent on a sufficient level of CalAccount enrollment. Table 5.2 summarizes our average estimates for projected enrollment rates under each policy option. Option 1 would likely have the lowest take-up rate of the three options, largely because of the lack of physical presence. Our projected enrollment for this option presents potential challenges for feasibility and a risk that uptake is not high enough to generate benefits that outweigh costs. However, Option 2 is expected to lead to higher levels of enrollment, and Option 3 is expected to have the highest take-up rate by offering more modes of access. Ultimately, the importance of in-person interaction for enrolling new customers likely goes back to the theme of gaining trust.

Table 5.1 | CalAccount Program Revenues, Midpoint Awareness ($ millions)

Year	Option 1	Option 2	Option 3
2026	$10.6	$12.7	$14.2
2027	$21.7	$26.0	$29.0
2028	$22.7	$27.1	$30.2
2029	$23.2	$27.7	$30.9
2030	$23.5	$28.0	$31.2
2031	$23.7	$28.3	$31.5
2032	$24.0	$28.6	$31.9
2033	$24.2	$28.9	$32.2
2034	$24.5	$29.2	$32.6
2035	$24.7	$29.5	$32.9

NOTE: Revenues are the sum of interchange fees generated from CalAccount card usage and fractional reserve lending. These revenues are based on midpoint awareness projections. These figures do not include the costs to the state or partnering financial institution and thus should not be used to assess CalAccount's profitability. More details on the fiscal impacts of CalAccount can be found in Annex II.

POTENTIAL IMPACTS OF THE CALACCOUNT PROGRAM

In Chapter 4, we analyze the trade-off between costs and benefits. Our estimations depend on detailed analyses along with specific assumptions shown in Appendixes C through F. Given that details on the implementation plan have yet to be specified, we crafted three policy options for CalAccount implementation. Table 5.3 describes each option, expected enrollment levels, and the size of the financial network and presents estimations of annualized values of benefits and costs in millions of dollars. In each option, the expected benefits marginally outweigh the expected costs of CalAccount.

A closer look at the expected benefits for CalAccount show real benefits for customers, especially Californians in marginalized groups. Unbanked and underbanked Californians who elect to participate in the CalAccount Program have the potential to benefit from savings by avoiding fees associ-

ated FDIC with banking and the use of alternative financial services. We estimate that annual savings could range from $41 to $101 per household for unbanked Californians and from $131 to $185 per household for underbanked Californians. Put in the broader context of poor financial well-being—just under two-thirds of Americans can cover an unexpected $400 expense—the annual costs savings estimated by our analysis may have meaningful impacts on households.[1]

Furthermore, we estimate that CalAccount could significantly reduce disparities in access to banking by race and ethnicity. Our analysis, built on data from survey responses and statistical estimations of uptake, suggests that the CalAccount Program could reduce the unbanked disparity between non-White and White households by 9 percent in a scenario with low awareness and as much as a third in a scenario with high awareness. We estimate that unbanked disparities between Hispanic and Non-Hispanic could be reduced by 10 percent with low awareness and 30 percent

Table 5.2 | Estimated Total CalAccount Enrollment, by Policy Option and Year in Operation

	Year 1	Year 2	Year 3	Year 4	Year 5	Year 6	Year 7
Option 1	296,443	595,762	598,843	602,357	605,556	608,490	610,899
Option 2	353,496	710,424	714,097	718,287	722,102	725,599	728,473
Option 3	393,469	790,758	794,848	799,510	803,758	807,651	810,849

SOURCE: Authors' analysis using data from the FDIC and RAND surveys.

NOTE: These projected enrollments are the primary estimates used in our model. For sensitivity analysis, we also predict enrollment under low- and high-awareness scenarios. See Appendix D for a detailed explanation of the different enrollment projections and their effects on the net social benefit of the program.

Table 5.3 | CalAccount Policy Options and Estimated Annualized Benefits and Costs ($ millions)

	Option 1: Mobile Banking	Option 2: Mobile Banking + Existing Brick-and-Mortar Financial Network	Option 3: Mobile Banking + Expanded Brick-and-Mortar Financial Network
Expected enrollments	Low	High	Highest
Size of financial network	Access to a robust and geographically expansive ATM network, with limited or no access to in-person banking	Access to a robust and geographically expansive ATM network, including bank or credit union branches	Access to a robust and geographically expansive ATM network, including bank or credit union branches plus additional state-designated locations
Annualized benefits	$114.9	$136.9	$152.2
Annualized costs	$111.5	$132.9	$151.0

with high awareness. And we estimate that the program could reduce the unbanked disparity between low income and non-low-income Californians by as little as 8 percent in the low-awareness scenario and as much as 31 percent in the high-awareness scenario.

STUDY LIMITATIONS AND KEY CONSIDERATIONS

This report aims to provide a comprehensive look at both the need for CalAccount and the feasibility of implementing the program as described in the California Public Banking Option Act. However, our assessment is not without limitations. For example, there may be approaches to implementing CalAccount beyond the three policy options we outline in Chapter 4. Our estimations of enrollment are ultimately limited by a high degree of uncertainty that, in part, depends on the structure of the program. Barriers to accessing banking services may extend beyond those that we intended to capture in our study design in collecting banking fees.

Our insight into banking fees paid by consumers and the potential benefits to a CalAccount bank partner are limited by the inability to access proprietary banking data. And our projections on enrollment may undercount the potential for attrition. However, one of the largest limitations of this study is our ability to answer *why* unbanked and underbanked Californians have limited interest in accessing banking services.

Above all, our insight into the role of trust is ultimately limited, showing a need for further analysis. The fact that the RAND survey reveals that a lack of trust for both banks and the state government is an issue for unbanked and underbanked Californians is, on one hand, not surprising. However, given the central importance of uptake for CalAccount feasibility, further analysis is needed to understand whether and how trust can be gained. Useful insight into the ability to gain trust in government-provided services may come from successful cases of gaining trust for vaccine delivery during the COVID-19 pandemic.

One of the largest limitations of this study is our ability to answer *why* unbanked and underbanked Californians have limited interest in accessing banking services.

RECOMMENDATIONS

Our findings suggest that the success of CalAccount hinges most on enrollment. If CalAccount does not reach a sufficient level of uptake, costs are likely to outweigh benefits. If it does, benefits are likely to outweigh costs, including meaningful savings for customers and significant reductions in unbanked disparities. Below, we conclude with a set of specific recommendations.

Recommendation 1: Implement CalAccount with Instant Payments

Mandating faster payments, which would provide account holders faster access to their funds, may reduce reliance on check-cashing services.[2] While not a formal part of this analysis, it is likely that adopting the use of fast payment systems—such as the Federal Reserve Banks' FedNow Service or The Clearing House's Real Time Payments Network—could bring further benefits to CalAccount customers. Fast payment systems are used by banks to process transactions instantly, with benefits extending to bank customers. Banks using fast payment systems can offer their customers immediate access to funds and real-time payment capabilities, 24 hours a day, seven days a week. Fast payment systems enable bank customers to make payments immediately, potentially avoiding late fees or service interruptions. Customers receiving funds through fast payment systems experience no delays in accessing or using those funds.[3]

Recommendation 2: Leverage Low-Cost Options for In-Person Services, Including Enrollment

Among the three policy options we considered for CalAccount, our findings show that a mobile banking-only option without the use of physical locations is unlikely to garner sufficient uptake for societal benefits to balance costs. This finding is supported by survey results showing increased interest in opening a bank account if it includes

The success of CalAccount hinges most on enrollment.

physical locations. However, given that we observed little disparity to accessing existing branch locations within urban areas but some disparity in rural areas and that survey respondents did not rank a lack of physical access as one of their primary reasons for being unbanked, the large costs of new branch locations may not be worth the benefit. Instead, access through ATM networks and existing branches may suffice. Where new locations are needed, particularly in rural areas, novel solutions, including the use of existing government facilities such as post offices and municipal buildings and the creative use of mobile bank branches by way of traveling vans, may extend access in a manner that increases uptake while managing potential costs.

Recommendation 3: Maximize Outreach Using Community Partners

Throughout this this chapter, we have come back to a common theme: Maximizing outreach is fundamentally important to the viability of CalAccount.[4] Only the high-awareness scenarios in our analysis achieved sufficient levels of enrollment for program sustainability: 879,000 for Option 1, 1 million for Option 2, and 1.2 million for Option 3. The associated costs of outreach are likely high (ranging from approximately $20 million to over $100 million), Furthermore, outreach can likely be maximized through partnerships with CBOs, faith-based organizations, and stakeholder groups.

Recommendation 4: Consider an Implementation Study

As CalAccount is implemented, our study points to several key areas in need of additional clarification and analysis:

- **Better understand trust issues and consider how to address them:** Where our study leaves off in identifying challenges for CalAccount enrollment, notably over trust, an implementation study could pick up. Focus groups could leverage survey responses to better understand whether mistrust for banks is based on unclear fees or negative experiences, whether social networks contribute, how endorsements from trusted partners alter perceptions, and how CalAccount's implementation may or may not overcome identified challenges.

- **Consider how best to integrate community partners:** Our interviews suggest the important role of CBOs, faith-based organizations, and stakeholder groups in rolling out CalAccount and maximizing uptake. An implementation plan could consider how to integrate these relationships.

- **Consider in greater detail structural issues that may affect CalAccount implementation:** An implementation study could refine revenue-sharing plans between the State of California and partner banks. It could clarify risk-based decisions on CIP, as well as consider whether accounts should have a cap at or below the $250,000 FDIC insurance limit. It could additionally decide on the use of nonbank, government-owned facilities for CalAccount branch operations, such as a pilot with the U.S. Postal Service.

NOTES

1   Board of Governors of the Federal Reserve System, *Economic Well-Being of U.S. Households in 2022*, May 2023a.

2   Ryan C. McDevitt and Aaron Sojourner, "The Need for Speed: Demand, Regulation, and Welfare on the Margin of Alternative Financial Services," *Review of Economics and Statistics*, January 2023.

3   Committee on Payments and Market Infrastructures, *Fast Payment: Enhancing the Speed and Availability of Retail Payments*, Bank for International Settlements, November 2016.

4   In Appendix D, we discuss Covered California as a useful example of a similar outreach effort.

Bibliography

AB 1177—*See* California State Legislature, California Public Banking Option Act.

Adams, Nevin E., "SCOTUS Scuttles CalSavers Challenge," National Association of Plan Advisors, March 1, 2022.

Agan, Amanda Y., and Michael D. Makowsky, "The Minimum Wage, EITC, and Criminal Recidivism," *Journal of Human Resources*, Vol. 58, No. 5, September 2023.

Aguila, Emma, Marco Angrisani, and Luisa R. Blanco, "Ownership of a Bank Account and Health of Older Hispanics," *Economics Letters*, Vol. 144, July 2016.

Akee, Randall, Maggie R. Jones, and Emilia Simeonova, "The EITC and Linking Data for Examining Multigenerational Effects," in Raj Chetty, John N. Friedman, Janet C. Gornick, Barry Johnson, and Arthur Kennickell, *Measuring Distribution and Mobility of Income and Wealth*, University of Chicago Press, October 2022.

Armey, Laura E., Jonathan Lipow, and Natalie J. Webb, "The Impact of Electronic Financial Payments on Crime," *Information Economics and Policy*, Vol. 29, December 2014.

Averett, Susan, and Yang Wang, "Effects of Higher EITC Payments on Children's Health, Quality of Home Environment, and Noncognitive Skills," *Public Finance Review*, Vol. 46, No. 4, July 2018.

Bachas, Pierre, Paul Gertler, Sean Higgins, and Enrique Seira, "How Debit Cards Enable the Poor to Save More," *Journal of Finance*, Vol. 76, No. 4, August 2021.

Baker, Scott R., Robert A. Farrokhnia, Steffen Meyer, Michaela Pagel, and Constantine Yannelis, "Income, Liquidity, and the Consumption Response to the 2020 Economic Stimulus Payments," *Review of Finance*, Vol. 27, No. 6, November 2023.

Bakker, Trevor, Nicole Kelly, Jesse Leary, and Éva Nagypál, "Data Point: Checking Account Overdraft," Consumer Financial Protection Bureau, July 2014.

Bank of North Dakota, "History of BND," webpage, undated. As of February 25, 2024:
https://bnd.nd.gov/history-of-bnd/

Bank On, "100 Coalitions," webpage, undated-a. As of October 31, 2023:
https://joinbankon.org/coalition-map/

Bank On, "Certified Accounts," webpage, undated-b. As of May 9, 2024:
https://joinbankon.org/accounts/

Bank On, "Get Certified: Join the National Bank On Movement," webpage, undated-c. As of May 29, 2024:
https://joinbankon.org/certify/

Bank On Coalition, *Playbook: Equipping Bank On Coalitions for Local Banking Access Success*, California Department of Financial Protection and Innovation, 2021.

Barr, Michael S., "Financial Services, Savings and Borrowing Among Low- and Moderate-Income Households: Evidence from the Detroit Area Household Financial Services Survey," *SSRN Electronic Journal*, March 2008.

Bastian, Jacob, and Katherine Michelmore, "The Long-Term Impact of the Earned Income Tax Credit on Children's Education and Employment Outcomes," *Journal of Labor Economics*, Vol. 36, No. 4, October 2018.

Berkeley Public Library, "Personal Finance at the Library, Appointments," webpage, March 23, 2021. As of May 17, 2024:
https://www.berkeleypubliclibrary.org/events/personal-finance-library-0

Birkenmaier, Julie, and Qiang Fu, "The Association of Alternative Financial Services Usage and Financial Access: Evidence from the National Financial Capability Study," *Journal of Family and Economic Issues*, Vol. 37, No. 3, 2016.

Birkenmaier, Julie, and Qiang Fu, "Household Financial Access and Use of Alternative Financial Services in the U.S.: Two Sides of the Same Coin?" *Social Indicators Research*, Vol. 139, 2018.

Board of Governors of the Federal Reserve System, "Regulation D: Reserve Requirements of Depository Institutions," *Federal Register*, Vol. 86, June 4, 2021.

Board of Governors of the Federal Reserve System, *Economic Well-Being of U.S. Households in 2022*, May 2023a.

Board of Governors of the Federal Reserve System, "The Federal Reserve Payments Study: 2022 Triennial Initial Data Release," webpage, July 27, 2023b. As of May 29, 2024:
https://www.federalreserve.gov/paymentsystems/fr-payments-study.htm

Board of Governors of the Federal Reserve System, "Regulation II (Debit Card Interchange Fees and Routing)," webpage, September 27, 2023c. As of May 29, 2024:
https://www.federalreserve.gov/paymentsystems/regii-about.htm

Board of Governors of the Federal Reserve System, *Community Bank Access to Innovation Through Partnerships*, October 2023d.

Board of Governors of the Federal Reserve System, "Annual Large Bank Capital Requirements," webpage, January 5, 2024a. As of May 29, 2024:
https://www.federalreserve.gov/supervisionreg/large-bank-capital-requirements.htm

Board of Governors of the Federal Reserve System, "Reserve Requirements," webpage, January 22, 2024b. As of October 31, 2023:
https://www.federalreserve.gov/monetarypolicy/reservereq.htm

Board of Governors of the Federal Reserve System, "Survey of Consumer Finances (SCF): Current Survey," webpage, April 5, 2024c. As of May 29, 2024:
https://www.federalreserve.gov/econres/scfindex.htm

Board of Governors of the Federal Reserve System, Division of Consumer and Community Affairs, "Regulation DD Background, Procedures, and Checklist," attachment to CA 09-14, "Updated Examination Procedures for Regulation DD," December 16, 2009.

Board of Governors of the Federal Reserve System, Federal Deposit Insurance Corporation, Financial Crimes Enforcement Network, National Credit Union Administration, and the Office of the Comptroller of the Currency, "Guidance to Encourage Financial Institutions' Youth Savings Programs and Address Related Frequently Asked Questions," U.S. Department of the Treasury, February 24, 2015.

Board of Governors of the Federal Reserve System, Federal Deposit Insurance Corporation, and the Office of the Comptroller of the Currency, "Interagency Overview of the Community Reinvestment Act Final Rule," fact sheet, October 2023.

Bonici, Max, and Michael Aphibal, "Harder, Better, Faster, Stronger: The New Interagency Rule for the Community Reinvestment Act," Venable LLP, November 2023.

Boyd-Swan, Casey, Chris M. Herbst, John Ifcher, and Homa Zarghamee, "The Earned Income Tax Credit, Mental Health, and Happiness," *Journal of Economic Behavior & Organization*, Vol. 190, Part A, June 2016.

Braga, Breno, Fredric Blavin, and Anuj Gangopadhyaya, "The Long-Term Effects of Childhood Exposure to the Earned Income Tax Credit on Health Outcomes," *Journal of Public Economics*, Vol. 190, October 2020.

Branas, Charles C., Eugenia South, Michelle C. Kondo, Bernadette C. Hohl, Philippe Bourgois, Douglas J. Wiebe, and John M. MacDonald, "Citywide Cluster Randomized Trial to Restore Blighted Vacant Land and Its Effects on Violence, Crime, and Fear," *Proceedings of the National Academy of Sciences*, Vol. 115, No. 12, February 2018.

Branton, Mike, and Tyler Spaid, "The Profitability of the Average Checking Account," *BankDirector*, April 22, 2013.

Brody, Jesse, Craig D. Miller, and Charles E. Washburn, Jr., "Top 5 Legal Considerations for FinTech Advertising," Manatt, Phelps & Phillips LLP, February 9, 2016.

Brown, James R., J. Anthony Cookson, and Rawley Z. Heimer, "Growing Up Without Finance," *Journal of Financial Economics*, Vol. 134, No. 3, December 2019.

Bunting, W. C., "The Impact of Data Mining on Information Disclosure by Regulatory Agencies: With an Application to Redlining," *Harvard Journal on Legislation*, Vol. 56, No. 2, Summer 2019.

Bureau of the Fiscal Service, "Direct Express® Program Financial Agent Selection Process: Requirements Document and Solicitation of Services," December 13, 2023.

Burke, Kathleen, Jonathan Lanning, and Jialan Wang, "Data Point: Payday Lending," Consumer Financial Protection Bureau, March 2014.

Bybee, Jared Ruiz, "Fair Lending 2.0: A Borrower-Based Solution to Discrimination in Mortgage Lending," *University of Michigan Journal of Law Reform*, Vol. 45, No. 1, Fall 2011.

"California Census 2020 Redistricting Blocks," ed. by ArcGIS: Esri, August 20, 2021. As of May 29, 2024: https://www.arcgis.com/home/item.html?id= 903453c84ade4f11aa3bce393af172d3

California Civil Code; Division 3, Obligations; Chapter 2, Hiring of Real Property; Section 1943, 2011.

California Code of Regulations, Title 1, Section, 2003, Methodology for Making Estimates.

California Department of Finance, "Projections," webpage, undated. As of April 18, 2024: https://dof.ca.gov/forecasting/demographics/projections/

California Department of Financial Protection and Innovation, "The Dual Chartering System and the Benefits of the State Charter," webpage, undated. As of May 17, 2024: https://dfpi.ca.gov/the-dual-chartering-system-and-the-benefits-of-the-state-charter/

California Department of Financial Protection and Innovation, "California Electronic Benefit Transfer (EBT) Project," webpage, August 28, 2019. As of February 1, 2024: https://dfpi.ca.gov/california-electronic-benefit-transfer-ebt-project/

California Department of Financial Protection and Innovation, *BankOn California*, 2021.

California Department of Financial Protection and Innovation, "Organizing a State Credit Union: Information Booklet," DFPI-391, Rev. 09-2023, September 2023.

California Department of Financial Protection and Innovation, "Credit Unions," webpage, March 15, 2024. As of May 17, 2024: https://dfpi.ca.gov/credit-unions/

California Department of General Services, *California State Contracting Manual*, Vol. 1, June 2023.

California Department of Human Resources, "Civil Service Pay Scale - Alpha by Class Title," 2020.

California Education Code, Title 3, Division 5, Part 42, Chapter 2, Article 19, Golden State Scholarshare Trust Act.

California Education Code, Title 3, Postsecondary Education; Division 5, General Provisions; Part 42, Student Financial Aid Program; Chapter 2, Student Financial Aid Programs; Article 19, Golden State Scholarshare Trust Act, Sections 69980–69994.

California Education Code, Title 3, Postsecondary Education; Division 5, General Provisions; Part 42, Student Financial Aid Program; Chapter 2, Student Financial Aid Programs; Article 19.5, California Kids Investment and Development Savings Program.

California Employment Development Department, "New: Changes to Your Debit Card," webpage, undated-a. As of February 1, 2024: https://edd.ca.gov/en/about_edd/the_edd_debit_card/

California Employment Development Department, "Quarterly Census of Employment and Wages (QCEW—About the Data)," database, undated-b. As of May 29, 2024: https://labormarketinfo.edd.ca.gov/data/ QCEW_About_the_Data.html

California Employment Development Department, "Size of Business Data for California: Second Quarter 2023," database, undated-c. As of May 29, 2024: https://labormarketinfo.edd.ca.gov/LMID/Size_of_Business_ Data_for_CA.html

California Government Code, Chapter 3.5, Administrative Regulations and Rulemaking.

California Government Code, Title 21, The CalSavers Retirement Savings Trust Act.

California Government Code, Title 21.1, CalAccount Blue Ribbon Commission.

California Public Banking Option Act—*See* California State Legislature, California Public Banking Option Act, AB 1177, October 4, 2021.

California State Controller's Office, "Volunteer Income Tax Assistance (VITA) Program," webpage, undated. As of May 17, 2024: https://www.sco.ca.gov/eo_vita.html

California State Legislature, California Public Banking Option Act, AB 1177, October 4, 2021.

California State Treasurer's Office, "California Secure Choice Retirement Savings Investment Board: Summary of Senate Bill 1234," October 24, 2016.

California State Treasurer's Office, "California Secure Choice Retirement Savings Investment Board: Governance Policies," July 22, 2019.

Campbell, Dennis F., Asís Martínez-Jerez, and Peter Tufano, "Bouncing Out of the Banking System: An Empirical Analysis of Involuntary Bank Account Closures," *Journal of Banking & Finance*, Vol. 36, No. 4, April 2012.

Carrell, Scott, and Jonathan Zinman, "In Harm's Way? Payday Loan Access and Military Personnel Performance," *Review of Financial Studies*, Vol. 27, No. 9, September 2014.

Célérier, Claire, and Adrien Matray, "Bank-Branch Supply, Financial Inclusion, and Wealth Accumulation," *Review of Financial Studies*, Vol. 32, No. 12, December 2019.

Célérier, Claire, and Purnoor Tak, "Exploiting Minorities Through Advertising: Evidence from the Freedman's Savings Bank," Department of Finance, Università Bocconi, October 17, 2022.

CFE Fund—See Cities for Financial Empowerment Fund.

CFPB—See Consumer Financial Protection Bureau.

Chalfin, Aaron, Benjamin Hansen, Jason Lerner, and Lucie Parker, "Reducing Crime Through Environmental Design: Evidence from a Randomized Experiment of Street Lighting in New York City," *Journal of Quantitative Criminology*, Vol. 38, March 2022.

Chang, Yunhee, "Does Payday Lending Hurt Food Security in Low-Income Households?" *Journal of Consumer Affairs*, Vol. 53, No. 4, Winter 2019.

Cheney, Julie S., and Sherrie L. W. Rhine, "How Effective Were the Financial Safety Nets in the Aftermath of Katrina?" *Consumer Interests Annual*, Vol. 52, 2006.

Chetty, Raj, John N. Friedman, and Jonah Rockoff, "New Evidence on the Long-Term Impacts of Tax Credits," *Proceedings of the 104th Annual Conference on Taxation*, 2011.

Chin, Aimee, Léonie Karkoviata, and Nathaniel Wilcox, "Impact of Bank Accounts on Migrant Savings and Remittances: Evidence from a Field Experiment," presentation, Western University, April 2011.

Christ, Carl F., "A Review of Input-Output Analysis," in *Input-Output Analysis: An Appraisal*, Princeton University Press, 1955.

Cities for Financial Empowerment Fund, "About Bank On," webpage, undated-a. As of May 20, 2024:
https://joinbankon.org/about/

Cities for Financial Empowerment Fund, "Bank On National Account Standards (2021–2022)," webpage, undated-b. As of May 29, 2024:
https://cfefund.org/bank-on-national-account-standards-2021-2022/

Cities for Financial Empowerment Fund, "Bank On National Account Standards (2023–2024)," fact sheet, undated-c.

City and County of San Francisco, "Get a Free SF City ID Card," webpage, May 15, 2023. As of May 17, 2024:
https://www.sf.gov/get-free-sf-city-id-card

City and County of San Francisco, Office of Financial Empowerment, "Open a Bank On Account," webpage, undated. As of May 17, 2024:
https://sfgov.org/ofe/openabankaccount#bankonpartners

City of Oakland, "General Information - Información General, Oakland City Identity Card," webpage, undated. As of May 17, 2024:
https://www.oaklandcityid.com/general-information--informacioacuten-general.html

City of Richmond, "Richmond Municipal Identification/Stored Value Card," webpage, undated. As of May 17, 2024:
https://www.ci.richmond.ca.us/2607/Richmond-Municipal-ID

Code of Federal Regulations, Title 31, Money and Finance: Treasury; Subtitle B, Regulations Relating to Money and Finance; Chapter X, Financial Crimes Enforcement Network, Department of the Treasury; Part 1020, Rules for Banks.

Collins, J. Michael, Sarah Halpern-Meekin, Melody Harvey, and Jill Hoiting, "'I Don't Like All Those Fees' Pragmatism About Financial Services Among Low-Income Parents," *Journal of Family and Economic Issues*, Vol. 44, No. 4, December 2023.

CommercialCafe, "Los Angeles Office Rent Price & Sales Report," webpage, undated.

Committee on Payments and Market Infrastructures, *Fast Payment: Enhancing the Speed and Availability of Retail Payments*, Bank for International Settlements, November 2016.

Conference of State Bank Supervisors, "Statutory Requirements for Opening Bank Accounts for Minors," webpage, August 23, 2021. As of October 31, 2023:
https://www.csbs.org/statutory-requirements-opening-bank-accounts-minors

Connecticut Green Bank, "Governance," webpage, undated. As of May 29, 2024:
https://www.ctgreenbank.com/about-us/governance/

Consumer Financial Protection Bureau, "Prepaid Product Agreements Database," webpage, undated. As of May 29, 2024:
https://www.consumerfinance.gov/data-research/prepaid-accounts/search-agreements/

Consumer Financial Protection Bureau, "Can I Get a Checking Account Without a Driver's License?" webpage, August 19, 2020. As of May 29, 2024, 2023:
https://www.consumerfinance.gov/ask-cfpb/can-i-get-a-checking-account-without-a-drivers-license-en-927/#

Consumer Financial Protection Bureau, "CFPB Targets Unfair Discrimination in Consumer Finance," March 16, 2022a.

Consumer Financial Protection Bureau, "Federal Regulators Fine Bank of America $225 Million over Botched Disbursement of State Unemployment Benefits at Height of Pandemic," July 14, 2022b.

Consumer Financial Protection Bureau, "CFPB Proposes Rule to Close Bank Overdraft Loophole That Costs Americans Billions Each Year in Junk Fees," January 17, 2024.

Conti-Brown, Peter, and Brian D. Feinstein, "Banking on a Curve: How to Restore the Community Reinvestment Act," *Harvard Business Law Review*, Vol. 13, No. 2, 2023.

Contra Costa County Employment and Human Services, "Electronic Benefits Transfer (EBT)," webpage, undated. As of May 17, 2024:
https://ehsd.org/benefits/calfresh-formerly-known-as-food-stamps/electronic-benefits-transfer-ebt/

Covered California, *Fiscal Year 2022–23 Budget*, June 16, 2022.

Covered California, "Covered California Finishes Open Enrollment with More Than 1.7 Million People Signed Up to Receive Quality Health Care Coverage," news release, March 9, 2023.

Dahl, Gordon B., and Lance Lochner, "The Impact of Family Income on Child Achievement: Evidence from the Earned Income Tax Credit," *American Economic Review*, Vol. 102, No. 5, August 2012.

Danitz, Brian, and Andrew F. Kirtley, "Claims Against Bank of America to Go Forward for Failing to Protect Unemployed Californians During Pandemic," Cotchett Pitre & McCarthy LLP, May 26, 2023.

Datatrac, "Deposit & Loan Acquisition Cost/ROI Calculator," webpage, undated. As of April 24, 2024:
https://solutions.datatrac.net/roicalculator

Demski, Joe, "Understanding IMPLAN: Direct, Indirect, and Induced Effects," *IMPLAN Blog*, June 18, 2020.

Desmond, Tyler, and Charles Sprenger, "Estimating the Cost of Being Unbanked," *Communities and Banking*, Federal Reserve Bank of Boston, Spring 2007.

Despard, Mathieu R., Shenyang Guo, Michal Grinstein-Weiss, Blair Russell, Jane E. Oliphant, and Anna deRuyter, "The Mediating Role of Assets in Explaining Hardship Risk Among Households Experiencing Financial Shocks," *Social Work Research*, Vol. 42, No. 3, September 2018.

DFPI—*See* California Department of Financial Protection and Innovation.

"Dibbs Taps Socure for 'Know Your Customer' Platform, Identity Verification," PYMNTS, April 5, 2022.

DiVito, Emily, *Banking for the People: Lessons from California on the Failures of the Banking Status Quo*, Roosevelt Institute, September 2022.

Du Bois, W. E. B., *The Souls of Black Folk*, Oxford University Press, 2009.

Duncan, Greg J., Pamela A. Morris, and Chris Rodrigues, "Does Money Really Matter? Estimating Impacts of Family Income on Young Children's Achievement with Data from Random-Assignment Experiments," *Developmental Psychology*, Vol. 47, No. 5, September 2011.

Edmiston, Kelly D., "Could Restrictions on Payday Lending Hurt Consumers?" *Economic Review*, Federal Reserve Bank of Kansas City, Vol. 96, January 1, 2011.

Eisenberg-Guyot, Jerzy, Caislin Firth, Marieka Klawitter, and Anjum Hajat, "From Payday Loans to Pawnshops: Fringe Banking, the Unbanked, and Health," *Health Affairs*, Vol. 37, No. 3, March 2018.

Esri Demographics Team, "California Census 2020 Redistricting Blocks," ArcGIS interactive map, accessed April 4, 2024. As of June 20, 2024:
https://www.arcgis.com/home/item.html?id=903453c84ade4f11aa3bce393af172d3#overview

Evans, William N., and Craig L. Garthwaite, "Giving Mom a Break: The Impact of Higher EITC Payments on Maternal Health," *American Economic Journal: Economic Policy*, Vol. 6, No. 2, May 2014.

Ewin, Brad, "ACH Fees—How Much Does ACH Cost?" ed. by Paul Foster, GoCardless, April 2023.

FDIC—*See* Federal Deposit Insurance Corporation.

Federal Deposit Insurance Corporation, "Deposit Market Share Reports—Summary of Deposits," webpage, undated. As of February 12, 2024:
https://www7.fdic.gov/sod/

Federal Deposit Insurance Corporation, "Bank Secrecy Act, Anti-Money Laundering, and Office of Foreign Assets Control," in *DSC Risk Management Manual of Examination Policies*, Section 8.1, December 2004.

Federal Deposit Insurance Corporation, *2021 FDIC National Survey of Unbanked and Underbanked Households*, 2021a.

Federal Deposit Insurance Corporation, *2021 FDIC National Survey of Unbanked and Underbanked Households: Appendix Tables*, 2021b.

Federal Deposit Insurance Corporation, "2021 FDIC National Survey of Unbanked and Underbanked Households," webpage, July 24, 2023. As of May 6, 2024:
https://www.fdic.gov/analysis/household-survey/index.html

Federal Deposit Insurance Corporation, "Quarterly Banking Profile: Fourth Quarter 2023," *FDIC Quarterly*, Vol. 18, No. 1, 2024.

Federal Financial Institutions Examination Council, "BSA/AML Examination Manual: Introduction," webpage, undated-a. As of May 29, 2024:
https://bsaaml.ffiec.gov/manual/Introduction/01

Federal Financial Institutions Examination Council, "Central Data Repository's Public Data Distribution," database, undated-b. As of May 23, 2024:
https://cdr.ffiec.gov/public/ManageFacsimiles.aspx

Federal Financial Institutions Examination Council, "NIC National Information Center," database, undated-c. As of January 29, 2024:
https://www.ffiec.gov/NPW

Federal Financial Institutions Examination Council, "Right to Financial Privacy Act," in *FDIC Consumer Compliance Examination Manual*, Section VIII, June 2006.

Federal Financial Institutions Examination Council, "Customer Identification Program," in *Bank Secrecy Act (BSA)/Anti-Money Laundering (AML) Examination Manual*, February 2021.

Federal Trade Commission, "How To Comply with the Privacy of Consumer Financial Information Rule of the Gramm-Leach-Bliley Act," July 2002.

Federal Trade Commission, "FTC Safeguards Rule: What Your Business Needs to Know," webpage, May 2022. As of May 23, 2024:
https://www.ftc.gov/business-guidance/resources/ftc-safeguards-rule-what-your-business-needs-know

Fekrazad, Amir, "Impacts of Interest Rate Caps on the Payday Loan Market: Evidence From Rhode Island," *Journal of Banking & Finance*, Vol. 113, April 2020.

FFIEC—*See* Federal Financial Institutions Examination Council.

FI Works, "Statistics," webpage, undated. As of April 24, 2024:
https://www.fiworks.com/resources/statistics

Financial Crimes Enforcement Network, "Interagency Interpretive Guidance on Customer Identification Program Requirements Under Section 326 of the USA PATRIOT Act," U.S. Department of the Treasury, April 28, 2005.

Fitzpatrick, Katie, "Does 'Banking the Unbanked' Help Families to Save? Evidence from the United Kingdom," *Journal of Consumer Affairs*, Vol. 49, No. 1, Spring 2015.

Fitzpatrick, Katie, "Bank Accounts, Nonbank Financial Transaction Products, and Food Insecurity Among Households with Children," *Journal of Consumer Affairs*, Vol. 51, No. 3, Fall 2017.

Foley, C. Fritz, "Welfare Payments and Crime," *Review of Economics and Statistics*, Vol. 93, No. 1, February 2011.

Fonte, Erin, "2017 U.S. Regulatory Overview of Mobile Wallets and Mobile Payments," *Wake Forest Journal of Business and Intellectual Property Law*, Vol. 17, No. 4, Summer 2017.

Foster, Kevin, Claire Greene, and Joanne Stavins, *2022 Survey and Diary of Consumer Payment Choice*, Federal Reserve Bank of Atlanta, No. 23-3, 2023.

Freedman, Matthew, and Emily G. Owens, "Low-Income Housing Development and Crime," *Journal of Urban Economics*, Vol. 70, No. 2, September–November 2011.

Friedline, Terri, and William Elliott, "Connections with Banking Institutions and Diverse Asset Portfolios in Young Adulthood: Children as Potential Future Investors," *Children and Youth Services Review*, Vol. 35, No. 6, June 2013.

Gabbard, Susan M., Richard Mines, and Jeffrey M. Perloff, "A Comparison of the CPS and NAWS Surveys of Agricultural Workers," Institute for Research on Labor and Employment, IRLE Working Paper 32-91, June 1991.

Garcia, Victor, "Counting the Uncountable, Immigrant and Migrant, Documented and Undocumented Farm Workers in California: Results from an Alternative Enumeration in a Mexican and Mexican-American Farm Worker Community in California and Ethnographic Evaluation of the Behavioral Causes of Undercount," U.S. Census Bureau, 1992.

General Statutes of Connecticut, Title 16, Public Service Companies; Chapter 283, Telephone, Gas, Power and Water Companies, Section 16-245n, Connecticut Green Bank, Charge Assessed Against Electric Customers, Clean Energy Fund, Environmental Infrastructure Fund.

Gennetian, Lisa A., Greg Duncan, Nathan A. Fox, Katherine Magnuson, Sarah Halpern-Meekin, Kimberly G. Noble, and Hirokazu Yoshikawa, "Unconditional Cash and Family Investments in Infants: Evidence from a Large-Scale Cash Transfer Experiment in the U.S.," National Bureau of Economic Research, Working Paper No. 30379, August 2022.

Getter, Darryl E., *Introduction to Financial Services: Credit Unions*, Congressional Research Service, IF11713, January 13, 2022a.

Getter, Darryl E., "Better, Together: Examining the Unified Proposed Rule to Modernize the Community Reinvestment Act," statement before the Committee on Financial Services, Subcommittee on Consumer Protection and Financial Institutions, U.S. House of Representatives, Congressional Research Service, 7-5700, July 13, 2022b.

Gjertson, Leah, "Emergency Saving and Household Hardship," *Journal of Family and Economic Issues*, Vol. 37, December 2014.

Gong, Cynthia, "Location, Location, Location: An Exploration of Geographic Disparities in Bank and Alternative Financial Service Access in Los Angeles County," University of California Los Angeles, June 26, 2023.

Greene, Meghan, Wanjira Chege, M. K. Falgout, and Necati Celik, *FinHealth Spend Report 2023: U.S. Household Spending on Financial Services Amid Historic Inflation and an Uncertain Economy*, Financial Health Network, June 2023.

Guzman, Gloria, and Melissa Kollar, *Income in the United States: 2022*, U.S. Census Bureau, P60-279, September 2023.

Hardy, Bradley L., "Income Instability and the Response of the Safety Net," *Contemporary Economic Policy*, Vol. 35, No. 2, April 2017.

Hayashi, Fumiko, "Cash or Debit Cards? Payment Acceptance Costs for Merchants," *Economic Review*, Federal Reserve Bank of Kansas City, Vol. 106, No. 3, August 2021.

Hayes, Joseph, Eric Assan, and Niu Gao, "California's Digital Divide," Public Policy Institute of California, fact sheet, April 2024. As of May 23, 2024:
https://www.ppic.org/publication/californias-digital-divide/

Hepler, Lauren, "Bank of America Says It Lost 'Hundreds of Millions' on California's Unemployment Fiasco," CalMatters, January 26, 2021a.

Hepler, Lauren, "How EDD and Bank of America Make Millions on California Unemployment," CalMatters, February 5, 2021b.

Hoory, Leeron, "Payroll Service Cost Guide (2024)," *Forbes Advisor*, April 21, 2024.

Horowitz, Ben, "Defining 'Low- and Moderate-Income' and 'Assessment Area,'" Federal Reserve Bank of Minneapolis, March 8, 2018.

Howard, Cory, "The Applicability of the BSA/AML Regulatory Regime to Indirect Lending Business Models," *Transactions: The Tennessee Journal of Business Law*, Vol. 19, No. 1, 2017.

Hoynes, Hilary, Doug Miller, and David Simon, "Income, the Earned Income Tax Credit, and Infant Health," *American Economic Journal: Economic Policy*, Vol. 7, No. 1, February 2015.

HR&A Advisors, *The Cost of Financial Exclusion: Understanding the Impact of the Unbanked in California*, May 2021.

HR&A Advisors, *The Case for CalAccount: A Statewide Solution for Equitable Financial Well-Being*, June 2024.

Internal Revenue Service, "Earned Income Credit (EIC)," Department of the Treasury, IRS Publication 596, December 20, 2022.

Internal Revenue Service, "Earned Income and Earned Income Tax Credit (EITC) Tables," webpage, November 13, 2023. As of December 12, 2023:
https://www.irs.gov/credits-deductions/individuals/earned-income-tax-credit/earned-income-and-earned-income-tax-credit-eitc-tables

Jacob, Brian A., Max Kapustin, and Jens Ludwig "The Impact of Housing Assistance on Child Outcomes: Evidence from a Randomized Housing Lottery," *Quarterly Journal of Economics*, Vol. 130, No. 1, February 2015.

Johnson, David S., Jonathan A. Parker, and Nicholas S. Souleles, "Household Expenditure and the Income Tax Rebates of 2001," *American Economic Review*, Vol. 96, No. 5, December 2006.

JPMorgan Chase, "How to Open a Bank Account for Non-U.S. Residents," webpage, undated. As of May 17, 2024:
https://www.chase.com/personal/banking/education/basics/us-bank-account-for-non-residents

Judicial Branch of California, "Collect Money from a Bank Account," California Courts Self-Help Guide, undated.

Judicial Council of California, "Exemptions from the Enforcement of Judgments," EJ-155, September 1, 2021.

Klein, Aaron, "'Everyone' Is the Wrong Way to Define Credit Union Members," Brookings Institution, July 12, 2017.

Koury, Renee, "EXCLUSIVE: BofA Says It Wants Out of Unemployment Benefits Contract as EDD Renews," ABC 7News, July 2, 2021.

Kuang, Jeanne, "California Missed Chances to Stop EBT Theft. It's Lost Tens of Millions of Taxpayer Dollars Since," CalMatters, November 8, 2023.

Kubrin, Charis E., and John R. Hipp, "Do Fringe Banks Create Fringe Neighborhoods? Examining the Spatial Relationship Between Fringe Banking and Neighborhood Crime Rates," *Justice Quarterly*, Vol. 33, No. 5, 2016.

Lachowska, Marta, "The Effect of Income on Subjective Well-Being: Evidence from the 2008 Economic Stimulus Tax Rebates," *Journal of Human Resources*, Vol. 52, No. 2, March 2017.

LaLumia, Sara, "The EITC, Tax Refunds, and Unemployment Spells," *American Economic Journal: Economic Policy*, Vol. 5, No. 2, May 2013.

Lavery, Diana, "Historical Redlining Data Now in ArcGIS Living Atlas," *ArcGIS Living Atlas* blog, Esri, August 7, 2020.

Leontief, Wassily, *Input-Output Economics*, Oxford University Press, 1986.

Levitin, Adam J., "The Financial Inclusion Trilemma," *Yale Journal on Regulation*, Vol. 41, January 2024.

LexisNexis, "Customer Identification Program," webpage, undated. As of May 23, 2024:
https://risk.lexisnexis.com/financial-services/financial-crime-compliance/customer-identification-program

Li, Zheng, "Equity of Urban Neighborhood Infrastructure: A Data-Driven Assessment," *Civil and Environmental Engineering Theses and Dissertations*, Southern Methodist University, Spring 2022.

Lohrentz, Tim, *The Net Economic Impact of Payday Lending in the U.S.*, Insight Center for Community Economic Development, March 2013.

Los Angeles County, "Center for Financial Empowerment," webpage, undated. As of May 17, 2024:
https://economicdevelopment.lacounty.gov/financial-empowerment/

Luthi, Ben, "What Is ChexSystems?" Experian blog, April 18, 2020.

Manoli, Day, and Nicholas Turner, "Cash-on-Hand and College Enrollment: Evidence from Population Tax Data and the Earned Income Tax Credit," *American Economic Journal: Economic Policy*, Vol. 10, No. 2, May 2018.

Marzahl, David, O. S. Owen, Steve Neumann, and Joshua Harriman, "First Accounts: A US Treasury Department Program to Expand Access to Financial Institutions," *Profitwise News and Views*, February 2006.

McDevitt, Ryan C., and Aaron Sojourner, "The Need for Speed: Demand, Regulation, and Welfare on the Margin of Alternative Financial Services," *Review of Economics and Statistics*, January 2023.

Melzer, Brian T., "The Real Costs of Credit Access: Evidence from the Payday Lending Market," *Quarterly Journal of Economics*, Vol. 126, No. 1, February 2011.

Metz, David, Benjamin M. Miller, Melissa Kay Diliberti, and Weilong Kong, *Guidelines for Conducting California Standardized Regulatory Impact Assessments*, RAND Corporation, RR-A1386-1, 2024. As of January 30, 2024:
https://www.rand.org/pubs/research_reports/RRA1386-1.html

Moebs, Mike, "What Does Your Checking Service Cost?" *Banking Exchange*, February 3, 2017.

Naceur, Sami Ben, Bertrand Candelon, Selim Elekdag, and Drilona Emrullahu, "Is FinTech Eating the Bank's Lunch?" IMF Working Papers, WP/23/239, November 2023.

Nacha, "Nacha Launches New Campaign Highlighting the Many People Benefiting from Direct Deposit," February 28, 2024.

Nagypál, Éva, "Data Point: Overdraft/NSF Fee Reliance Since 2015—Evidence from Bank Call Reports," Consumer Financial Protection Bureau, December 2021.

National Association of Federally-Insured Credit Unions, "Back to Basics: Membership and Par Value," *Compliance Blog*, March 27, 2017a.

National Association of Federally-Insured Credit Unions, "Back to Basics: Are All Members Created Equal?" *Compliance Blog*, July 31, 2017b.

National Conference of State Legislatures, "Security Breach Notification Laws," webpage, January 17, 2022. As of May 29, 2024:
https://www.ncsl.org/technology-and-communication/security-breach-notification-laws

National Credit Union Administration, homepage, undated. As of October 31, 2023:
https://ncua.gov/

National Credit Union Administration, "FAQs: Final CIP Rule," RA2004-04Encl, 2004. As of June 3, 2024:
https://bsaaml.ffiec.gov/docs/resources/NCUA_DOCs/RA2004-04_and_Enclosure.pdf

National Credit Union Administration, "Interagency Interpretive Guidance on Customer Identification Program Requirements Under Section 326 of the USA PATRIOT Act," April 28, 2005. As of May 15, 2024:
https://www.fincen.gov/resources/statutes-regulations/guidance/interagency-interpretive-guidance-customer-identification

National Credit Union Administration, "Field-of-Membership Expansion," December 13, 2021.

National Credit Union Administration, "Low-Income Designation," February 29, 2024a.

National Credit Union Administration, "Call Report Quarterly Data," database, March 12, 2024b. As of September 1, 2023:
https://ncua.gov/analysis/credit-union-corporate-call-report-data/quarterly-data

National Credit Union Administration, "Choose a Field of Membership," May 17, 2024c.

NCUA—*See* National Credit Union Administration.

Office of Governor Gavin Newsom, "California IDs for All," September 23, 2022.

Office of Inspector General, *Fiscal Service Needs to Improve Program Management of Direct Express*, U.S. Department of the Treasury, OIG-14-031, March 26, 2014.

Office of the Assistant Secretary for Planning and Evaluation, *Guidelines for Regulatory Impact Analysis*, U.S. Department of Health and Human Services, 2016.

69

Office of the Attorney General, California Department of Justice, "Check Casher Permit Program," webpage, undated-a. As of May 23, 2024:
https://oag.ca.gov/casher

Office of the Attorney General, California Department of Justice, "Your Financial Privacy Rights," webpage, undated-b. As of May 23, 2024:
https://oag.ca.gov/privacy/facts/financial-privacy/rights

Office of the Comptroller of the Currency, "Bank Secrecy Act (BSA)," webpage, undated-a. As of October 31, 2023:
https://www.occ.treas.gov/topics/supervision-and-examination/bsa/index-bsa.html

Office of the Comptroller of the Currency, "Privacy," webpage, undated-b. As of October 31, 2023:
https://www.occ.treas.gov/topics/consumers-and-communities/consumer-protection/privacy/index-privacy.html

OMB—See U.S. Office of Management and Budget.

Palmer, Caroline, David C. Phillips, and James X. Sullivan, "Does Emergency Financial Assistance Reduce Crime?" *Journal of Public Economics*, Vol. 169, January 2019.

Parker, Jonathan A., Nicholas S. Souleles, David S. Johnson, and Robert McClelland, "Consumer Spending and the Economic Stimulus Payments of 2008," *American Economic Review*, Vol. 103, No. 6, October 2013.

Parolin, Zachary, Elizabeth Ananat, Sophie M. Collyer, Megan Curran, and Christopher Wimer, "The Initial Effects of the Expanded Child Tax Credit on Material Hardship," Working Paper No. 29285, National Bureau of Economic Research, September 2021.

Philippon, Thomas, "On Fintech and Financial Inclusion," BIS Working Papers, No. 841, February 2020.

Public Law 105-219, Credit Union Membership Access Act, August 7, 1998.

Ray, Rashawn, and Hoda Mahmoudi, *Systemic Racism in America: Sociological Theory, Education Inequality, and Social Change*, Routledge, 2022.

Rhine, Sherrie L. W., and William H. Greene, "Factors That Contribute to Becoming Unbanked," *Journal of Consumer Affairs*, Vol. 47, No. 1, Spring 2013.

Robb, Cliff A., Patryk Babiarz, Ann Woodyard, and Martin C. Seay, "Bounded Rationality and Use of Alternative Financial Services," *Journal of Consumer Affairs*, Vol. 49, No. 2, Summer 2015.

Rocha, Erika, and Gabriela Herrera, "Salinas' Health Struggles as Manifestations of Historical Processes: A Report on the History of Health of Salinas Residents," *Pathways: Stanford Journal of Public Health*, Vol. 1, No. 1, May 2023.

Rodriguez-Sanchez, Jose Ivan, "An Economic Lifeline? How Remittances from the US Impact Mexico's Economy," Rice University's Baker Institute for Public Policy, November 13, 2023.

Rostad, Whitney L., Joanne Klevens, Katie A. Ports, and Derek C. Ford, "Impact of the United States Federal Child Tax Credit on Childhood Injuries and Behavior Problems," *Child Youth Services Review*, Vol. 107, February 2019.

Servon, Lisa J., and Antonieta Castro-Cosío "Reframing the Debate About Financial Inclusion: Evidence from an Up Close View of Alternative Financial Services," paper prepared for the Federal Reserve Economic Mobility Conference, Federal Reserve Bank of St. Louis, March 5, 2015.

Shevlin, Ron, "Why People Don't Switch Banks Anymore," *Forbes*, May 1, 2019.

Sprague, Aleta, "Next Generation TANF: Reconceptualizing Public Assistance as a Vehicle for Financial Inclusion," *University of the District of Columbia Law Review*, Vol. 18, No. 1, March 2015.

Starr, Darriya, Joseph Hayes, and Niu Gao, "Broadband Access Has Grown in Recent Years, but Many Still Lack Access," Public Policy Institute of California, June 2023.

State of California, California Government Code Sections 11364–11365 and Participation, 2005.

Stulz, René M., "FinTech, BigTech, and the Future of Banks," *Journal of Applied Corporate Finance*, Vol. 31, No. 4, Winter 2022.

Tax Policy Center, "State and Local Tax Policies," in *Briefing Book*, Urban Institute and Brookings Institute, January 2024.

Thomson, Rachel M., Erik Igelström, Amrit Kaur Purba, Michal Shimonovich, Hilary Thomson, Gerry McCartney, Aaron Reeves, Alastair Leyland, Anna Pearce, and S. Vittal Katikireddi, "How Do Income Changes Impact on Mental Health and Wellbeing for Working-Age Adults? A Systematic Review and Meta-Analysis," *Lancet Public Health*, Vol. 7, No. 6, June 2022.

Tuttle, Cody, "Snapping Back: Food Stamp Bans and Criminal Recidivism," *American Economic Journal: Economic Policy*, Vol. 11, No. 2, May 2019.

U.S. Bank, "Matrícula Consular Mexicana," webpage, undated. As of May 17, 2024:
https://www.usbank.com/bank-accounts/matricula-consular-mexicana.html

U.S. Bureau of Labor Statistics, "Consumer Expenditure Survey Results on the 2008 Economic Stimulus Payments (Tax Rebates)," webpage, April 9, 2018. As of December 13, 2023:
https://www.bls.gov/cex/taxrebate.htm

U.S. Bureau of Labor Statistics, "Table 7. Private Industry Workers by Census Region and Division," December 2023, in *Employer Costs for Employee Compensation*, March 13, 2024a. As of May 23, 2024:
https://www.bls.gov/news.release/ecec.t07.htm

U.S. Bureau of Labor Statistics, "May 2023 State Occupational Employment and Wage Estimates: California," in *Occupational Employment and Wage Statistics*, database, April 3, 2024b. As of April 3, 2024:
https://www.bls.gov/oes/current/oes_ca.htm

U.S. Census Bureau, Geography Division, "Metropolitan Areas," in *Geographic Areas Reference Manual*, Chapter 13, Economics and Statistics Administration, U.S. Department of Commerce, November 1994.

U.S. Code, Title 15, Chapter 41, Subchapter III, Credit Reporting Agencies, Section 1681 et seq., Fair Credit Reporting Act.

U.S. Code, Title 31, Subtitle IV, Chapter 53, Subchapter II, Records and Reports on Monetary Instruments Transactions.

U.S. Office of Management and Budget, Circular A-4, "Regulatory Analysis," November 9, 2023.

Varjavand, Reza, "Growing Underground Economy: The Evidence, the Measures, and the Consequences," *Journal of International Management Studies*, Vol. 11, No. 3, 2011.

Ventura County Library, "Financial Empowerment Class," webpage, undated. As of May 17, 2024:
https://www.vencolibrary.org/library-events/financial-empowerment-class-1007231030

Veterans Benefits Administration, "Opening an Account at a Financial Institution for Veterans Without Permanent Housing," fact sheet, U.S. Department of Veterans Affairs, undated.

Wright, Richard, Erdal Tekin, Volkan Topalli, Chandler McClellan, Timothy Dickinson, and Richard Rosenfeld, "Less Cash, Less Crime: Evidence from the Electronic Benefit Transfer Program," *Journal of Law and Economics*, Vol. 60, No. 2, May 2017.

Yuan, Zhen, *Impact of Cares Act Stimulus on Consumption: Evidence from Zip Code Level Transactions*, thesis, University of Chicago, August 2021.

Zhang, David Hao, "How Do People Pay Rent?" Federal Reserve Bank of Boston, Research Data Report No. 16-2, June 13, 2016.

Zinman, Jonathan, "Restricting Consumer Credit Access: Household Survey Evidence on Effects Around the Oregon Rate Cap," *Journal of Banking & Finance*, Vol. 34, No. 3, March 2010.